Vegetable Gardening

Vegetable Gardening

Jo Whittingham

LONDON, NEW YORK, MUNICH, MELBOURNE, DELHI

SENIOR EDITOR Zia Allaway
ACTING SENIOR DESIGNER Rachael Smith
MANAGING EDITOR Anna Kruger
MANAGING ART EDITOR Alison Donovan
DTP DESIGNER Louise Waller
PICTURE RESEARCH Lucy Claxton,
Richard Dabb, Mel Watson
PRODUCTION CONTROLLER Rebecca Short

PRODUCED FOR DORLING KINDERSLEY
Airedale Publishing Limited
CREATIVE DIRECTOR Ruth Prentice
PRODUCTION MANAGER Amanda Jensen

PHOTOGRAPHY Sarah Cuttle, David Murphy

First American Edition, 2007

Published in the United States by
DK Publishing, 375 Hudson Street,
New York, NY 10014

09 10 11   10 9 8 7 6 5 4 3 2

A Cataloging-in-Publication record for this book is
available from the Library of Congress.

ISBN-13: 978-0-7566-2692-1

ISBN-10: 0-7566-2692-7

DK books are available at special discounts for bulk
purchases for sales promotions, premiums, fund-raising, or
educational use. For details, contact: DK Publishing Special
Markets, 375 Hudson Street, New York, NY 10014 or
SpecialSales@dk.com

Reproduced by Colourscan, Singapore
Printed and bound by Star Standard, Singapore

Discover more at
www.dk.com

Contents

Growing your own

Whether you have a garden, a patio, or a windowsill, you can grow your own delicious fresh vegetables. Fast-maturing crops make decorative displays in pots and look fabulous when combined with flowers, while a potager-style plot brimming with ornamentals and edibles is ideal for a small garden. Use these and other ideas featured in this chapter to inspire your planting, so you can enjoy your vegetables before they even reach your plate.

Combining vegetables and flowers

Small gardens need to look their best year round and usually have no room for a separate vegetable garden, but with a little imagination, the forms and colors of vegetables can look striking alongside flowers and produce a tasty harvest, too.

Pictures clockwise from top far left

Crop circles Planting crops to form decorative patterns is a great way to add interest and it needn't take up much space. Here, a central tree is surrounded by a circular bed of herbs, then concentric rings of salad leaves, carrots, onions, and additional herbs, with paths in between for easy access. Make the most of the colorful varieties of lettuce available to brighten up the garden and the salad bowl.

Squash edging Vigorous, trailing plants, such as these squashes, might seem too large for a small garden. However, if they are trained along the front of an established border, or even over mature shrubs, their bold yellow flowers, dramatic foliage, and colorful fruit look great spilling over onto the path. Add plenty of organic matter to the soil in established borders to provide the vegetables with sufficient nutrients to grow well.

Ornamental display A simple sowing of summer annuals creates a vibrant, meadowlike effect surrounding a carefully planned bed of purple- and blue-green-leaved vegetables. As well as looking good, the daisylike flowers will attract many beneficial insects to the plot to pollinate crops and prey on pests. Cabbages, leeks, and different varieties of kale will continue the display through fall and winter.

Bumper harvest Climbing vegetables are ideal where space is limited because they will produce a big crop from a small patch of soil. In this border, a wigwam of runner beans towers over dwarf French beans and the feathery foliage of carrots, while nasturtiums, yellow marigolds, and a pot of petunias add welcome color. The silvery, thistlelike foliage of perennial globe artichokes gives permanent structure to the border, while its flower buds make a delicious dish.

Container harvest

It is possible to grow a huge range of vegetables and herbs successfully in pots, which means that anyone with a patio, balcony, or even just a sunny windowsill can harvest their own fresh produce for the kitchen.

Pictures clockwise from top left

Ranks of terra-cotta pots Large terra-cotta pots are stylish, easy to care for, and look perfect arranged along the edge of a flight of steps or on a patio. This patch of light shade suits sage, mint, thyme, and parsley well, although almost any herb will flourish in a container when well watered. To keep plants compact and bushy, regularly pinch out the growing tips or clip with shears.

Recycled kitchen colander Hanging baskets are a great way to create extra growing space, and a kitchen colander, with ready-made drainage holes, is a quirky alternative to standard designs. Tumbling varieties of bush tomatoes, with trusses of colorful fruit, will cascade over the edge of the container, as will fast-growing orange-flowered nasturtiums. Herbs, such as parsley and thyme, are perfect for filling in any gaps. Hang the basket out of strong winds and keep it well watered.

Space-saving plantings In a small garden, it is even more important to get the most out of all the available space, so choose large containers and grow fast-maturing crops, such as lettuce, with slower-growing vegetables. Here red-leaved lettuces, planted around a zucchini, are ready for harvest, while the zucchini plant still has a long fruiting season ahead of it. The neighboring sweet pepper plant shares its pot with a fine specimen of basil.

Grouped containers Be imaginative and use containers of all shapes, sizes, and finishes, and arrange them in groups to create an exciting and colorful effect. This tiled patio is given a modern feel with metallic containers filled with the bold foliage of Asian greens and colored stems of Swiss chard 'Bright Lights'. All kinds of improvised pots work well, including galvanized garbage cans or colorful plastic containers, provided that drainage holes are drilled in their bases.

Horizontals and verticals

Taking time to plan a vegetable garden before you plant can pay dividends throughout the season. Clever use of low rows and tall accent plants creates microclimates that different vegetables enjoy, as well as great visual effects.

Pictures clockwise from right

Alternate rows Many gardeners admire the long, uniform rows of traditional large vegetable gardens, but they can also be useful in the smaller garden. If rows are planted running along the length of the garden away from the house, they draw the eye onward and make the garden appear longer. In this garden, curved rows of lettuce, chard, onions, and zucchini are interspersed with dense lines of marigolds (*Tagetes*), which effectively combine to lengthen the appearance of the border. Marigolds are often grown alongside vegetables because their strong scent is thought to confuse insect pests seeking particular crop plants.

Climbing screens When trained up a straight row of canes or trellis, climbing vegetables, such as these runner beans, make effective, fast-growing screens, which can have many uses in the garden. Such a screen could be used to separate a vegetable garden from the rest of the garden, or to disguise compost piles or garbage cans. All kinds of trailing plants, including cucumbers and squashes, can be trained to cover unsightly walls or fences. Climbing beans are easily damaged by high winds, so if a windbreak is required, perennial Jerusalem artichokes would be a better choice.

Compact planting Where space for growing vegetables is limited, it makes sense to grow crops in tightly packed rows, where as little soil as possible is left bare. Here, the contrasting leaf forms of different lettuce varieties look attractive next to a row of ferny carrot foliage and backed by tall sweet corn. This compact planting has disadvantages—you need to leave sufficient space to access the crops, and taller plants can shade out shorter ones—but the advantages include fewer weeds, due to less bare soil, and shade from the sweet corn, which benefits the lettuces in summer.

Block planting in beds

An easy way to grow crops is in beds, where the gardener can focus on improving the soil, removing weeds, and planting dense blocks of vegetables in a manageable, defined area.

Pictures clockwise from top left

Model of efficiency One big advantage of growing crops in beds is that the whole bed can be reached from the path. This means that the soil does not get trampled and no space has to be left between plants for access, allowing crops, such as these leeks, to be grown closer together in efficient blocks.

Decorative and practical Specially constructed brick beds are ideal for tiny gardens because they look decorative, and even very narrow beds can still support useful crops of herbs, salad leaves, and, where the soil is deep enough, as it is here, parsnips.

Low-maintenance kitchen garden This garden demonstrates that using beds makes it easier to keep paths weed-free, and you need add organic matter only to the soil that will be used for growing. Crops can also be weeded and picked without getting muddy shoes.

Raised beds for easy cultivation

Not only do raised beds bring interesting height and structure to a garden design, they also elevate the level of the soil to make cultivation and harvesting your vegetables much less strenuous.

Pictures clockwise from top left

Raised bed of salad crops A simply constructed raised bed that has been filled with good quality topsoil, improved with plenty of compost, is the perfect place for growing herbs and unusual leaf crops, such as mustard 'Red Giant' and red orach. These cut-and-come-again crops can be cut with a pair of scissors and then rushed back to the kitchen for the freshest leaves.

Sun-lovers' paradise For many gardeners, not having to bend or kneel to weed and harvest crops is a real bonus. Building a substantial raised bed against a sunny wall or fence, as illustrated, means that heat-loving crops, such as tomatoes, will thrive and require less watering than those growing in pots.

Easy pickings These high brick raised beds would suit less mobile gardeners and make an attractive, permanent feature in any garden. This bush tomato variety has ample space to grow over the edge of the bed, where the fruit will create a colorful display and be at the perfect height to pick with ease.

Weeding in comfort The decorative edging on this raised bed doubles as seating, making weeding around the densely planted lettuces, carrots, and onions a relaxing, sit-down job rather than a chore. Cordon tomatoes trained up the fence make great use of a small space and give a lush feel to this area of the garden.

Growing vegetables under cover

Vegetable plants often need protection from cold weather and persistent pests, particularly when they are young and most vulnerable. Being prepared with the appropriate equipment and protective covers is the best way to avoid losses.

Pictures clockwise from left

Keeping pests at bay Netting supported on wire hoops prevents pigeons from feasting on young brassicas. A finer mesh will also keep out butterflies, whose eggs hatch into hungry caterpillars.

Protecting winter leaves Salads, such as these dark red lettuces and Asian greens, respond well to the protection from cold, wet weather that a cold frame provides, allowing them to be grown all through the winter.

Greenhouse effect This greenhouse is bursting with seedlings to be hardened off and potted on. Even in a small garden, a greenhouse can be worthwhile, providing valuable space for raising seeds and achieving earlier harvests.

Shielding tomato plants Outdoor-grown tomatoes can be hardened off and shielded from cold nights in an inexpensive plastic greenhouse, which conveniently houses a standard-sized growing bag.

Where to start

Creating your own vegetable garden may seem a little daunting, but by carefully selecting a suitable area for your garden, and discovering the type of soil you have, you will bring success a bit closer. Start off with easy crops, such as salads, radishes, and herbs, and increase your range as your confidence grows. This chapter will help you understand more about your chosen vegetables and the conditions they require, and also outlines the equipment and tools you will need before you start.

Choosing a site

Growing vegetables in ideal conditions is not always possible, particularly if you have limited space, but it pays to find a sunny spot that is sheltered from the wind and easily accessible for watering and weeding.

Sheltered or sunny walls

A wall that faces the sun provides plants with protection from the wind and reflects the sun's heat back onto your crops during the day. It will also absorb heat and release it at night when the air temperature falls. A sheltered microclimate is ideal for growing heat-loving vegetables, such as tomatoes, eggplants, and peppers, so if you have one in your garden, make the most of it. Improve the soil, create a raised bed, or position pots at the base of the wall. Remember to keep plants well watered.

Tips for sunny walls
- Add supports, such as wire mesh, to the wall to secure tall and scrambling plants as they grow.
- Take advantage of a sunny wall as the perfect backdrop for tomatoes in a growing bag.
- Be adventurous and try growing more unusual crops, such as sweet corn and chili peppers.

Small vegetable beds

Make the most of a small space by planning your crops carefully and squeezing as much variety into the plot as possible. Many vegetables are attractive plants in their own right, but add extra color to the beds by including some flowers, too, which will not only look good but also help attract pollinating insects. Planting vegetables close together also means that there is little bare soil on which weeds can establish, helping to minimize maintenance, but crop yields may be slightly reduced.

Tips for small vegetable beds
- Densely planted vegetables need rich soil, so work in plenty of organic matter in fall.
- Choose vegetable varieties with interesting colors and forms to add drama to your beds.
- Be wary of planting too close to tall hedges, which cast shade and take moisture from the soil.

A greater range of vegetables can be grown by a sunny wall.   Rows of vegetables packed tightly together will suppress weeds.

Growing under cover

Protecting crops from cold and wet weather in a greenhouse, cold frame, or under cloches gives them a head start in spring, extends the growing season into fall, and allows a range of tender vegetables to be grown that may not perform well outdoors. Fitting large structures into a small garden can be difficult, so consider whether you have a suitable site before buying costly equipment. Site greenhouses and frames in full sun, away from overhanging trees, but sheltered from the wind as much as possible. Plants under cover rely on the gardener to provide adequate water and temperature control, which can amount to a lot of work, so make sure you have the time.

Tips for growing under cover
- Control greenhouse ventilation to regulate temperatures and remove damp air that can encourage disease. Automatic ventilation is a good investment.
- Use cold frames and mobile cloches for raising seedlings and protecting young plants.
- Where there is no space outdoors, try sowing seeds and growing heat-loving crops on a sunny windowsill.
- Install a water supply, such as a rain barrel, next to the greenhouse to make life easier.

Container growing

Filling pots, troughs, and window boxes with a range of vegetables is one of the best ways for those with little or even no garden to harvest their own, homegrown produce. Tomatoes, salads, dwarf beans, herbs, and some root vegetables are just a few of the crops that will thrive in containers and can make attractive displays on patios, steps, and windowsills. Containers filled with good-quality potting mix are also useful in gardens with very poor soil or where soil-borne pests and diseases make vegetable growing difficult. However, containers can be expensive to buy and fill with potting mix, and without regular watering and fertilizing, plants will not perform well, so consider the practicalities before you begin.

Tips for container growing
- Keep costs down and be creative by making your own pots from galvanized metal bins or plastic containers.
- Good drainage is vital to prevent soil from becoming waterlogged, so be sure pots have holes in their bases.
- Choose large pots, as they hold more soil, take longer to dry out, and suit many vegetables well.
- Look for vegetable varieties suited to container growing, such as short, round carrots.

It is crucial to choose a site in full sun for your greenhouse.

Colorful crops, like this chard, are easy to grow in pots.

Knowing and improving your soil

The structure, fertility, drainage, and acidity (pH) of your soil all have an impact on the health of the plants. Knowing what type of soil you have and how to improve it will help you to create the best growing environment.

Soil health and fertility Good soil drains well but retains plenty of moisture that roots can access. It is easy to dig and full of organisms, such as earthworms, beetles, bacteria, and fungi. Organic matter is a vital component of soil and is broken down by tiny organisms to release nutrients and improve the soil's water-holding capacity. Healthy, fertile soil is a rich dark brown, but whatever the color of yours, improve it by digging in organic matter, such as compost and manure, or applying it every year as a surface mulch over well-watered, moist soil.

Knowing your soil's pH The pH scale measures the degree of soil acidity, which determines the availability of nutrients, as well as the presence of beneficial soil organisms and less desirable soil-borne diseases. Low numbers on the pH scale indicate acidic soil; pH 7 is

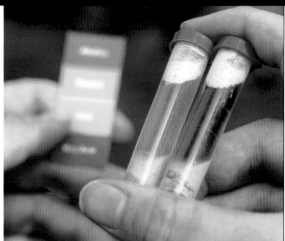

A simple soil testing kit will reveal the pH of your soil, so you will know whether it is acidic or alkaline.

neutral; higher numbers show an alkaline soil. Garden soils normally fall between pH 4.5 and pH 7.5, but the ideal for vegetables is pH 6.5. Lime can be applied to increase the pH, but it is more difficult to lower it. Soil testing kits are widely available and easy to use. Simply mix a soil sample in a test tube as directed, and compare the color of the solution to the chart to determine the pH.

Determining the soil's texture

The size of the mineral particles in soil determines its texture, which tells you how it should be treated during cultivation. There are three basic soil types—clay, silt, and sand—which occur in varying proportions. Pick up some of your soil and squeeze; when moist, clay soil forms sticky clumps and is shiny when smoothed; light, sandy soil falls through your fingers; and fine silt feels silky. Clay soil holds water and nutrients well but can have poor drainage and be heavy to work. Sandy soil is light to dig, but dries out and loses nutrients rapidly.

Lighten heavy clay soil by adding grit.   Add organic matter to sandy soil to help it retain moisture.

Digging in organic matter Improve the structure of soil by digging in bulky organic matter every year. This is most beneficial on sandy soils, where it helps to retain moisture and nutrients that are otherwise quickly lost. Adding organic matter along with grit to clay soils can help open up the soil structure and improve its sticky texture.

Well-rotted garden compost is a valuable form of organic matter, but well-rotted farmyard manure, spent mushroom compost, and green manures are all useful alternatives. During a dry spell in fall or winter, spread a 4–6-in (10–15-cm) layer of organic matter over the soil and dig it in to a spade's depth. Alternatively, sow a green manure, such as mustard (*see right*), cut it down before it becomes woody, leave to wilt, then dig into the soil.

Adding a surface mulch Mulching is simply placing a layer of bulky organic matter or a plastic sheet over the soil surface. This practice is beneficial because it prevents moisture from evaporating from the soil surface, controls the soil temperature, and inhibits the germination of weed seeds. Organic mulches are also drawn into the soil by earthworms, where they break down and improve the soil structure. Garden compost, well-rotted manure, spent mushroom compost, and straw can all be used as mulch and should be applied in a generous layer around plants. Leave gaps around plant stems, though, otherwise rot can set in, and apply the mulch to moist soil because it is more difficult for water to penetrate the thick covering and wet dry soil.

Liming acidic soils By adding lime, you can increase the pH of acidic soil to make it better suited to vegetable growing. Crushed chalk or ground limestone are the safest and cheapest forms of lime to use. Apply them at the recommended rate for your type of soil; clay soils require heavier applications than sandy soils to achieve the same effect.

Treat the soil in fall or winter, at least four weeks after adding any bulky organic matter. Divide the plot into 1-sq-yd (1-sq-m) sections with string lines. Wearing gloves, long sleeves, safety glasses, and a mask, weigh out the correct amount of powder to treat 1 sq yd (1 sq m). Sprinkle this evenly onto the soil with a spade, repeat until the whole plot is covered, then rake the lime into the soil.

Knowing and improving your soil *continued*

Skimming weeds Tidy up weed-covered ground by skimming annual weeds off the surface and burying them in a trench. Remove any perennial weeds first, then shallowly slide the spade under the surface to lift the weeds in sections. Dig a trench in the area that you have cleared and lift the sections of weedy soil into it, so that the weeds are upside down. This process can be repeated across a large area and the weeds will break down in the trench and improve the soil.

Use a spade to skim annual weeds.   Turn skimmed weeds into a trench.

Single digging This is the usual way to cultivate and add organic matter to the soil. Spread a layer of organic matter over the whole plot, to be incorporated as you dig. Dig a trench about 12 in (30 cm) wide, to one spade's depth, across the plot and take the soil to the far end of the plot in a wheelbarrow. Use soil from a second trench, dug next to the first and to the same dimensions, to fill the first trench. Continue the process across the plot, until the soil moved from the first trench is used to fill the last.

Double digging On a new site with deep topsoil, dig a trench 2 ft (60 cm) wide to a depth of two spades, and add some organic matter to it. Move the soil to the end of the plot. Dig a second trench of the same size next to the first—use the soil to fill the first trench. Add organic matter to the second trench, and repeat these steps across the whole plot. If you have thin soil, dig to just one spade's depth and fork the bottom to a further spade's depth to avoid bringing infertile subsoil up to the surface.

Achieving a fine tilth for sowing
A level soil surface with a fine crumbly texture, without large stones or old plant material, gives seeds and young plants the best start. This can be achieved by lightly drawing a metal-headed rake over previously dug soil in one direction, then again at 90° to the first raking.

Applying fertilizer Good soil preparation prior to planting should supply plants with adequate nutrients, but for newly cultivated or poor soil, it may be necessary to apply a top-dressing of fertilizer while plants are growing. Fertilizers contain nitrogen (N), phosphorus (P), and potassium (K) in various ratios, so check the products available and choose one that suits your needs. Wear gloves when handling fertilizers and apply them at the recommended rate—excess nutrients can be harmful to plants. Scatter fertilizer evenly over the rooting area of the crop and avoid dropping any on the leaves because it could scorch them. Incorporate into the soil surface using a push hoe.

Making compost

Every gardener should find space for a compost pile or bin, as it turns garden and kitchen waste into a valuable source of organic matter to dig into soil or use as a mulch.

The final product Compost should be dark brown with a crumbly texture and pleasant, soil-like smell. The decomposition of bulky organic materials requires oxygen, moisture, and the right balance of carbon- and nitrogen-rich waste (*opposite*), which means that careful management is necessary. However, a successful compost pile is easy to achieve.

Different compost bin designs Your first task is to find a compost bin that suits the size of your garden and the amount of waste to be broken down. It is best to have two bins, to allow the contents of one to be aerated by turning it into a second bin, which means that a new pile can be started in the first. The type of bin you choose depends on appearance, space, and cost considerations, but ensure that it has a loose-fitting cover to prevent waterlogging. Place your bin on bare soil, add compostable material, and let nature do the rest.

Wooden bins look good and can be bought or homemade. Choose a design with removable front slats for easy turning.

Plastic bins are relatively cheap and simple to install, but their design means that turning the contents can be tricky.

Bins constructed from wire mesh are particularly suitable for composting fallen leaves to make leafmold.

What goes on the pile? Almost all plant waste from the garden can be composted, except for diseased material, perennial weeds, and meat and cooked waste, which attracts vermin. Nitrogen-rich (green) waste aids decomposition, but this must be balanced with carbon-rich (brown) waste to open up the structure of the pile and allow air to circulate. Aim to add a 50:50 mix of green and brown waste to your pile during the year.

What to add

- Carbon-rich woody prunings and hedge trimmings (which usually need to be shredded), plant stems, fall leaves, shredded newspaper and cardboard.
- Nitrogen-rich grass cuttings, herbaceous plant material, weeds, vegetable plants, fruit and vegetable peels, tea bags, coffee grounds.

Carbon-rich brown material adds bulk.   Chop up woody material before adding.

Making a compost trench

Kitchen waste, such as fruit and vegetable peels, tea bags, and eggshells can also be composted in a long trench. The trench is best made during the fall, when large areas of soil are often bare and the waste has time to break down before planting begins in spring. Vigorous plants, such as runner beans and squashes, respond particularly well to the high nutrient levels provided by kitchen leftovers.

Dig a trench about 12 in (30 cm) wide to one spade's depth and fill it with alternate layers of waste and soil. Then add a layer of soil on top. Allow at least two months before planting over the trench. As with any composting method, do not include meat or cooked waste because it may attract vermin.

Scatter waste on the bottom of the trench.   Fill with alternate layers of soil and waste.

Water-wise gardening

Droughts and water metering can cause problems during hot, dry summers, but the solution is to know how to use resources efficiently and to store your own supplies.

Keeping plants healthy Plants in dry soil are susceptible to disease and yield less, so it pays to keep soil moist. Watering thoroughly so the moisture penetrates deep into the soil is better than wetting the surface daily. Water in the evening or early morning to minimize evaporation.

Storing rainwater Water can be collected from the roofs of houses, garages, sheds, and greenhouses, and stored in rain barrels that have spigots at their bases. These supplies of rainwater are a valuable alternative to city water or well water, although during hot summer months, rainfall rarely keeps up with demand.

Rain barrels are often easier to install in a convenient part of the garden than running a hose to the area. Make sure that you set your rain barrel on a stack of bricks, slabs, or a specially made base, to allow a watering can to fit under the spigot. Although many gardeners dislike the appearance of plastic barrels, they are easy to disguise with ornamental planting, such as grasses and bamboo (*right*), or tall rows of runner beans.

Using gray water Water that has already been used in the home is usually suitable for watering plants in the garden. Normal household soaps and detergents do not damage plants, but avoid bleaches and strong disinfectants. Allow hot water to cool before applying it to the soil.

Water the roots Pour water around the stem base, beneath the plant's foliage, so that it is absorbed into the soil around the roots where it is needed. The shade of the foliage also helps to prevent evaporation, and neighboring weeds are not inadvertently watered, too.

The essential tool kit

While a good-quality set of tools will not do the work for you, they certainly make gardening tasks easier and more enjoyable than attempts made using inferior or unsuitable products.

Everything in its place The essential tools are normally considered to be a spade, fork, hand fork, trowel, hoe, and pruners. Kept in good condition, they can last for years, so find a safe, dry place to store them, and clean and sharpen them regularly.

Spades and forks

These stalwarts are probably used every time you garden, for digging, planting, and harvesting, among many other things. It is, therefore, worth investing in the best that you can afford. Make sure that you find the handle and shaft length comfortable.

- **Standard spade** With its large 11-x-8-in (28-x-20-cm) blade, this is good for working large areas efficiently.
- **Border spade** A smaller blade makes this lighter to work with and suitable for digging in small gardens.
- **Digging fork** With four 12-in- (30-cm-) long prongs (tines), this is the ideal tool for heavy cultivation.
- **Border fork** With four shorter and narrower tines, this is lighter than a digging fork and perfect for tight spaces.

Break up soil with a fork.

Earth up potatoes with a spade.

Rakes and hoes

These tools are used for preparing the soil for planting and keeping weeds under control. You can buy single handles with clip-on heads if storing lots of tools is a problem.

- **Metal rake** Long-handled, with a head about 12 in (30 cm) wide and short prongs. Use to prepare a fine tilth.
- **Wooden rake** Clear and level soil with the wooden-toothed head of this rake, which should be about 30 in (75 cm) wide.
- **Push hoe** Push the sharp, flat blade shallowly through the soil to sever weeds' top growth from their roots.
- **Swan-necked draw hoe** Pull this hoe toward you in short movements to uproot weeds. You can also use it for marking seed drills.

Clear weeds with a draw hoe.

Create a fine tilth with a rake.

Planting tools

Delicate tasks involving seedlings and young plants require smaller tools, so that you can avoid damaging them, and the work is less awkward. Try to buy tools that you find comfortable and easy to use, so that you can enjoy this less physically demanding work.

- **Hand fork** Usually three-pronged with either a wooden or plastic handle. Find a sturdy one for planting and weeding.
- **Trowel** The perfect tool for digging planting holes. Trowel blades are always short, but can vary in width.
- **Dibber** Useful for pricking out seedlings and making small planting holes. They can be made of plastic, metal or wood.

Mark out drills with a trowel.   Prick out using a dibber.

Canes and netting

Supporting tall vegetable plants and those that climb naturally prevents them from sprawling along the ground, helps them stand up to strong winds, presents the crop at a convenient height for picking, and looks great.

- **Bamboo canes** Arrange in wigwams or rows for climbing beans, and use to support any tall crops weighed down with fruit or in a windy spot.
- **Pea sticks** A row of hazel or birch twigs makes the perfect climbing frame for a double row of peas.
- **Chicken wire** Light wire mesh, supported by canes, is ideal for pea plants to curl their tendrils around.
- **Nylon netting** Use to protect crops from birds and rodents, and even butterflies if the mesh is fine.

Beans climb rows of canes.   Chicken wire supports peas.

Cloches

Protect young plants and enjoy earlier crops with cloches. Glass cloches insulate plants most effectively, but plastic versions are cheaper and less likely to break.

- **Plastic tunnel cloches** Ideal for protecting whole rows, these light cloches are easy to move but need to be well secured once in place.
- **Homemade cloches** The top halves of clear plastic beverage bottles make ideal cloches because the open tops provide good ventilation.
- **Glass lantern cloches** Handsome and practical, the lid can be lifted and turned to allow air to circulate inside.
- **Plastic bell cloches** These must be pegged down to stop them from blowing away, but are versatile and cheap.

Tunnel cloches suit long rows.   Homemade cloches are effective.

Cloches and cold frames

Protect crops from pests and bring on their growth in cold weather by covering them with cloches or growing them in permanent cold frames.

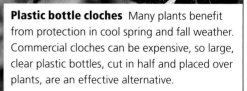

Plastic bottle cloches Many plants benefit from protection in cool spring and fall weather. Commercial cloches can be expensive, so large, clear plastic bottles, cut in half and placed over plants, are an effective alternative.

Corrugated plastic cloches Whole rows of plants can be covered using long, low tunnel cloches, which are left open at the ends for thorough ventilation or closed off when greater protection is required. No rain will reach cloched plants, so remember to water them as necessary.

Rigid plastic cloches These large cloches are ideal for protecting blocks of young plants or more substantial crops, such as zucchini or early potatoes. The warm, dry atmosphere is also perfect for drying onion crops after harvest. Anchor these light structures to the ground.

Cold frames Usually permanent structures of brick with framed glass "lights," cold frames are useful for hardening off young plants and extending the productive season of crops such as salads and zucchini. Constructed in a sheltered, sunny spot, they are a good alternative to a greenhouse in a small garden, with the angled lights allowing water to run off and the maximum amount of light to reach the plants. A frame with a hard base is suited to acclimatizing pot-grown plants to outdoor temperatures, while a bed of improved soil allows crops to be grown in the frame. Prop the lights open during the day to provide ventilation, and keep plants inside well watered.

Using a greenhouse

Start crops early and obtain better yields with the aid of a greenhouse, which will raise the air temperature and can, if heated, protect plants from frost.

Damping down In hot summer weather, plants wilt if the air is too dry. Counteract this by damping down the floor and staging in the greenhouse with a watering can on hot days, to raise the humidity levels.

Temperature control Since plants suffer in a greenhouse that is too hot, and young leaves can be scorched in bright sunlight, use some form of shading during summer. A cheap and effective method is to apply a coat of shading wash to the outside of the greenhouse in early summer. You can then wash it off in late summer when the heat of the sun is less intense. Sheets of fine mesh are also available. These can be attached to the outside of the greenhouse, although they are less effective than shading washes.

To keep your greenhouse frost-free, install a heater specially designed for greenhouses. Electric fan heaters with thermostats are a good option; employ an electrician to install the necessary electricity supply.

Apply shading wash in summer.

Attach shading mesh to lower temperatures.

Effective ventilation Even in winter, greenhouses need ventilation to remove damp air, but in summer it is vital to ventilate well to control the temperature. Vents in the roof allow hot air to escape, while low side vents admit fresh, cooler air from outside; open both to achieve good circulation, but reduce ventilation during cool nights.

Extra shelf space In spring, greenhouse staging can be packed with trays and pots of germinating seeds and young plants waiting to be moved outside. When they are planted out, however, the staging often takes up valuable space. Shelves that fold down to make way for the main greenhouse crops are a useful solution to this problem.

Planning your crops

When faced with a vast choice of vegetables and only a small garden to plant them in, it is difficult to decide what to grow. However, if you spend time planning how to use your space, you can squeeze in an amazing variety.

Grow the right crops Tempted by all sorts of exotic vegetables, gardeners sometimes forget to grow what they enjoy eating. Wonderful as it is to have a fine crop of kale or kohlrabi, if you hate the taste of them, then your efforts have been wasted. On the other hand, if you struggle to find more unusual vegetables and herbs at the store, then grow what you need yourself. Crops that are simple to grow, such as runner beans and purple sprouting broccoli, are often expensive to buy, so it makes sense to grow what you would normally pay a premium for.

Use space efficiently Make the most of every patch of soil by drawing up a plan of how long each crop will be in the ground and what could be ready to plant after it. Intercropping, shown below with tomatoes and lettuces, is a great way to squeeze a fast-growing crop in between slower-growing plants before they fill their allotted space. Small beds easily reached from the path can be planted in tightly packed blocks because there is no need to step on the soil. In this way, more plants fit into a given space and productivity increases.

Intelligent growing Take account of your soil and climatic conditions before you start planting; these affect what will grow successfully, so it makes sense to work with, rather than against, them. In cold regions, it may be worth investing in a greenhouse or cold frame, or raising early and heat-loving crops on a warm windowsill or in a conservatory. To ensure a consistent supply of many vegetables, try sowing small numbers of seeds successionally every two or three weeks, so that they reach maturity over a long period.

Lettuces are ideal for sowing between slower-growing tomatoes, as they will be harvested before the tomatoes need more space.

A three-bed crop rotation system

Crop rotation Vegetables can be divided into three main groups according to their needs: root vegetables, peas and beans, and brassicas. Traditionally, the members of each group are grown together and rotated, in order, around three beds. Different crops have different soil and nutrient needs, and rotating them helps to create the right environment for each type. For example, peas and beans fix nitrogen in the soil, so are followed by nutrient-hungry brassicas. Root crops need lower nitrogen levels, so do well after brassicas and break up the soil for deep-rooting peas and beans. The squash family, fruiting vegetables, and salads can be grown with any of the groups.

Why bother? Crop rotation is worthwhile even in a small garden because when crops are grown in the same place year after year, pests and diseases can accumulate and cause serious problems. Moving crops every year reduces the likelihood that this will occur and also helps regulate soil pH because only brassicas may need added lime.

Bed one
- Year one: root crops. Incorporate plenty of organic matter before planting.
- Year two: peas and beans. Prepare soil with generous amounts of manure or compost.
- Year three: brassicas. Lime acidic soil and dig in more well-rotted compost.

Bed two
- Year one: peas and beans. Improve the soil with lots of manure or compost.
- Year two: brassicas. Add good quality-compost and lime acidic soil to control clubroot.
- Year three: root crops. Prepare the soil by digging in more organic matter.

Bed three
- Year one: brassicas. Apply compost and the correct quantity of lime to acidic soils.
- Year two: root crops. Add more compost to keep soil in good condition.
- Year three: peas and beans. Apply well-rotted manure to help retain moisture and add nutrients.

Root crops

Easy to grow and indispensable in the kitchen, most root crops simply need to be sown outdoors and kept free of weeds to do well. With carefully selected varieties and successional sowing, you can harvest roots all year.

How to grow

Site and soil Many root crops appreciate well-drained, slightly acidic soil that still holds organic matter and some of the nutrients dug in for a previous crop. However, potatoes crop best on recently manured soil, and brassica root crops (radishes, rutabagas, and turnips) may succumb to clubroot in acidic soils that have not been limed. Stony soils may cause malformation of long-rooted crops.

Sowing and planting out Most root crops are grown from seed, sown from early spring into outdoor seedbeds. Sow seed into drills at the appropriate depth (*see table below*), cover with soil, and water in. Sow carrots, beets, turnips, and radishes successively every few weeks for a continuous supply. Seed potatoes are actually tubers, which should be left to sprout (chit) in a cool, light place before planting into a deep drill or individual holes.

Care and potential problems Thin seedlings out, leaving strong plants to grow on at the correct spacing. Keep the surrounding soil weed-free and moist, watering as necessary in dry spells. Protect potato plants from frost and cover their lower stems and leaves with soil (earth up) as they grow. Potatoes often suffer from blight in damp weather. Carrots, parsnips, and brassicas are also prone to certain pests and diseases (*see pp.112–115*). Employ measures to minimize the risk of attack and also try growing resistant varieties.

Harvest and storage Most roots can be left in the ground until needed, although they should be protected from frost. Lift potatoes by early fall, allow them to dry for a few hours, and store in paper sacks in a cool dark place.

Sowing depths and spacing

CROP	SOWING DEPTH	SPACING	
		Plants	Rows
Potato, early	4 in (10 cm)	12 in (30 cm)	16 in (40 cm)
Potato, maincrop	4 in (10 cm)	15 in (38 cm)	30 in (75 cm)
Beet	1 in (2.5 cm)	4 in (10 cm)	10 in (25 cm)
Carrot	½ in–¾ in (1–2 cm)	4 in (10 cm)	6 in (15 cm)
Parsnip	¾ in (2 cm)	6 in (15 cm)	10 in (25 cm)
Radish	½ in (1 cm)	1 in (2.5 cm)	6 in (15 cm)
Rutabaga	¾ in (2 cm)	8 in (24 cm)	14 in (35 cm)
Turnip	¾ in (2 cm)	4 in (10 cm)	10 in (25 cm)

Carrots freshly harvested from the ground.

Cultivation tips

Protecting against carrot flies A 24-in (60-cm) barrier of very fine netting, fleece, or plastic, stretched around secure posts and buried at the base, is sufficient to keep carrot flies at bay (*left*). The females fly close to the ground and are unable to reach the carrots to lay their eggs.

Roots in pots Carrots, beets, and radishes all grow happily in containers at least 10 in (25 cm) wide and deep (potatoes need larger pots), as long as they are kept well watered. This is a good way to start the earliest crops under cover.

Growing potatoes through black plastic If earthing up potatoes sounds like too much effort, try planting your crop through holes cut in a layer of thick black plastic—push the edges into the soil to secure the plastic in place. This keeps out the light and helps warm the soil for a fast-maturing crop.

Crops to choose

Potato Early varieties suit small gardens since they are harvested by midsummer, whereas maincrops tie up the soil until mid-fall.

Beet Not all beets are red, so you can choose unusually colored varieties and opt for bolt-resistant types for early sowings.

Parsnip These roots will stand in the soil through winter with a covering of straw, but seeds need to be sown the previous spring.

Radish Sow radishes successively for crops over a long season. Exotic hardy winter radishes can also be sown in summer.

Brassicas

Encompassing many of the hardiest winter crops, including cabbages and Brussels sprouts, that will see you through lean times, this group also includes many summer favorites and Asian greens, such as mizuna.

Healthy cabbages ready for harvesting.

How to grow

Site and soil Moist, well-drained, fertile soil suits most brassicas, so it is best to work in plenty of organic matter well in advance of planting. Lime should be added to soil with a pH lower than 6.8 to prevent clubroot, and it is sensible to rotate crops to prevent buildup of the disease in the soil. Firm soil keeps the plants stable in winter weather, so do not dig the bed deeply before planting. Brassicas prefer full sun, but will tolerate partial shade, while taller plants, such as Brussels sprouts, need to be staked on windy sites.

Sowing and planting out Most brassicas are best sown into an outdoor nursery bed or modules under cover in spring, and transplanted into their final positions as young plants. However, sow summer sowings of calabrese and kohlrabi directly into seedbeds in their final positions.

Care and potential problems Brassicas are cool-weather crops and tend to bolt during hot, dry spells. Water transplants daily and mature plants once a week in dry weather. Watch for early signs of pests and diseases. The cabbage root fly is common and lays its eggs on all brassicas, so take preventative measures with all seedlings. Cover the plants with fleece to prevent butterflies from laying their eggs. Slugs, snails, aphids, and whiteflies all enjoy brassicas, and pigeons may destroy winter crops. Take measures to avoid clubroot (*see above*).

Harvest and storage Hardy winter and spring crops will stand well in the garden and can be harvested at any point, but eat summer crops fresh, before they bolt.

Sowing depths and spacing

CROP	SOWING DEPTH	SPACING	
		Plants	Rows
Cabbage—spring	¾ in (2 cm)	10 in (25 cm)	12 in (30 cm)
summer/fall	¾ in (2 cm)	18 in (45 cm)	18 in (45 cm)
winter	¾ in (2 cm)	18 in (45 cm)	24 in (60 cm)
Cauliflower	¾ in (2 cm)	18 in (45 cm)	24 in (60 cm)
Brussels sprouts	¾ in (2 cm)	24 in (60 cm)	24 in (60 cm)
Calabrese	¾ in (2 cm)	8 in (24 cm)	12 in (30 cm)
Sprouting broccoli	¾ in (2 cm)	24 in (60 cm)	24 in (60 cm)
Kale	¾ in (2 cm)	18 in (45 cm)	18 in (45 cm)
Kohlrabi	¾ in (2 cm)	9 in (23 cm)	12 in (30 cm)

Cultivation tips

Netting against pigeons Winter brassica crops are a favorite with hungry pigeons. Preempt their feast and protect plants by covering the brassica bed with netting (*see left*) secured to stakes or wires that are sturdy enough to last through winter weather.

Thwarting cabbage root flies Female flies lay their eggs at the base of young plants, so buy collars, or make your own out of thick paper or carpet underlay, to prevent this. Use 6-in (15-cm) squares of your chosen material and cut a slit in the center of each, so that it can be placed snugly around the base of the plant.

Coming back for seconds Broccoli and calabrese continue to produce secondary spears after the central one is cut, and frequent harvesting encourages even more to be produced. When harvesting summer cabbages, leave 2-in (5-cm) stumps and cut a cross ½ in (1 cm) deep in the top of them. This encourages a loose head of leaves to develop, giving you a second crop.

Crops to choose

Cauliflower Best in rich, heavy soils with plenty of manure. Snap outer leaves over each curd to protect them from sun and frost.

Kale Hardy and tolerant of poor soil, kale is easy to grow. Colorful, textured varieties brighten up the winter garden.

Brussels sprouts Harvest this classic winter vegetable from the base of the stem upward, by snapping off each sprout by hand.

Kohlrabi Eat the swollen stems of these fast-growing exotics in salads or stir-fries. Harvest when no larger than a tennis ball.

Alliums

This group includes onions, leeks, and garlic. All are strongly flavored and simple to grow on free-draining soils. It is difficult to imagine cooking without them, and all have great health benefits, so why not grow your own?

How to grow

Site and soil A sunny, open site with fertile, well-drained soil is ideal for members of the onion family because they are prone to fungal diseases in damp conditions. Treat soil with a pH of less than 6.5 with lime, and don't grow them in the same place year after year. Manure the ground a few months in advance to prevent too much soft growth.

Sowing and planting out All alliums, except garlic, can be grown from seed. Sow in modules in early spring under glass for early crops, or outdoors for later crops. Harden off seedlings grown indoors, and plant out at the desired spacing, or thin direct-sown rows. The final spacing dictates the harvest size of the bulbs. Transplant leek seedlings when they are pencil-size. Drop them into holes 6 in (15 cm) deep and the width of a spade shaft. Water well, but do not backfill with soil. Succession-sow green onions. Onions and shallots can also be planted as sets (and garlic as cloves); these small bulbs mature faster and are less prone to disease than seed-grown plants. Place sets 4 in (10 cm) apart in shallow drills. Water if the soil is very dry.

Care and potential problems Water onions and shallots in very dry weather. Leeks respond well to regular watering and mulch. Keep the ground weed-free. All alliums are susceptible to fungal diseases, including onion white rot, downy mildew, and fusarium. Maintain good air circulation around plants and well-drained soil to minimize problems, and remove infected material. Seedlings are more susceptible to damage by onion flies than sets.

Harvest and storage Harvest leeks and green onions when green, but allow the leaves of onions, shallots, and garlic to yellow and die down before lifting them. Store onions, shallots, and garlic on a wire rack until the leaves rustle; then hang them in a cool, dry place.

A healthy crop of leeks, just out of the ground

Sowing depths and spacing

CROP	SOWING DEPTH	SPACING	
		Plants	Rows
Onions	¾ in (2 cm)	2–4 in (5–10 cm)	12 in (30 cm)
Shallots	1 in (2.5 cm)	6–8 in (15–20 cm)	10 in (25 cm)
Garlic (cloves)	2–4 in (5–10 cm)	4 in (10 cm)	12 in (30 cm)
Leeks	1 in (2.5 cm)	6 in (15 cm)	12 in (30 cm)
Green onions	½ in (1 cm)	½ in (1 cm)	6 in (15 cm)

Cultivation tips

Planting maincrop onions
From late winter to early spring, press sets into a shallow drill, so their tips just show when firmed in.

Harvesting once leaves have died down Be patient and allow the leaves of onions, shallots, and garlic to die down naturally before harvesting them from late summer to early fall. If you intend to store the bulbs, don't be tempted to fold the leaves down, which speeds up their withering, because it could damage the necks of the onions. Lift the harvest carefully with a fork to avoid any bruising that might allow rot to set in later.

Crops to choose

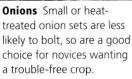

Onions Small or heat-treated onion sets are less likely to bolt, so are a good choice for novices wanting a trouble-free crop.

Shallots A single shallot set will divide to produce a crop of several small, sweet bulbs, which are expensive in stores.

Garlic Do not plant supermarket cloves; you will achieve better yields using virus-free stock of cooler-climate varieties.

Green onions A quick, easy onion, ideal for the gaps between slower-growing crops. Try one of the unusual red varieties.

Legumes

Pea and bean crops require less fertilizer than other vegetables because their roots are home to bacteria that take nitrogen from the air and fix it in the soil. Leave the nutrient-rich roots to break down in the soil after harvest.

Sugar snap peas ready for harvesting.

How to grow

Site and soil These climbing plants do best in full sun on fertile, slightly alkaline soil, improved with plenty of organic matter. Since they are susceptible to similar pests and diseases, practice crop rotation (*see pp.38–39*). Fava beans prefer clay soils, while other peas and beans do best on lighter soils. Provide shelter from strong winds.

Sowing and planting out All legume seeds need warm soil in which to germinate, so wait until mid-spring to sow outdoors or start them off under cloches or in pots indoors. Successional sowings help to ensure a steady supply of produce. Erect appropriate supports before sowing or planting out to avoid damaging young plants.

Care and potential problems Beans are commonly grown up wigwams or rows of canes held together with string; peas scramble up chicken wire supported by canes or twiggy pea sticks. Beans may need coaxing up and tying into their supports, while peas hold on with tendrils.
　Keep plants well weeded, and mulch if possible. There is no need to water before flowering, unless plants are wilting. Begin watering generously when flowering starts, to encourage pods to set. For bushier plants, pinch out growing tips when plants reach the top of their supports.
　Rodents love legume seeds, so sow indoors where this is a problem. Protect crops from pea moths by covering with fleece. Infestations of aphids are also common.

Harvest and storage Peas and beans are at their tastiest when small and freshly picked, so harvest frequently; this also encourages greater yields. Eating quality deteriorates quickly, even when crops are refrigerated, so either use right away or freeze any excess as soon after harvest as possible. Borlotti beans can be left on the plant to mature, then dried and stored in a cool, dark place.

Sowing depths and spacing

CROP	SOWING DEPTH	SPACING	
		Plants	Rows
Fava beans	3 in (8 cm)	10 in (25 cm)	12 in (30 cm)
French beans, dwarf	2 in (5 cm)	4 in (10 cm)	18 in (45 cm)
climbing	2 in (5 cm)	6 in (15 cm)	18 in (45 cm)
Runner beans	2 in (5 cm)	6 in (15 cm)	18 in (45 cm)
Peas	1½ in (4 cm)	4 in (10 cm)	18–24 in (45–60 cm)

Cultivation tips

Discouraging blackflies on fava beans Blackflies are fond of the young, sappy growth at the tips of fava bean plants. Deter them by pinching out the tips when plants have plenty of flowers and the first pods have set.

Supporting runner beans Climbing French and runner beans need the support of sturdy canes, ideally at least 7 ft (2.2 m) tall, to hold up their lush growth. Wigwams of six or eight canes tied at the top are easy to construct.

Crops to choose

Colorful peas With violet flowers and pods, the snow pea 'Ezethas Krombek Blauwschok' adds color to the productive garden.

Fava beans Rarely available fresh in stores, these delicious beans are easy to grow and can be sown in fall for a welcome late spring crop.

French beans Dwarf varieties of this heavy-cropping legume suit the small garden very well. They thrive in pots to yield plenty of gourmet beans.

Borlotti beans Grown in the same way as a climbing French bean, this beautiful Italian variety has pink-flecked pods. Eat the beans fresh or use them dried.

Cucurbits

Vigorous and high-yielding, these plants, which include pumpkins, zucchini, and cucumbers, are great fun to grow.

Trailing varieties look great scrambling up a fence or over an arch, which makes them easier to fit in a small garden.

How to grow

Site and soil Plants in the pumpkin family come from hot climates and thrive on well-drained soil improved with organic matter. Once established, their growth is rapid and extensive, so leave them enough space. Cucumbers and zucchini do well in pots or growing bags.

Sowing and planting out These tender plants cannot tolerate frost and will not germinate or grow in the cold. Sow seeds indoors, in biodegradable pots to prevent root disturbance, and plant seedlings out when the weather improves. Harden seedlings off before planting out, after the last frost. If nights are cool, cover with a cloche.

Care and potential problems Cucurbits require lots of watering. Outdoor and greenhouse cucumbers, and summer and winter squashes, often benefit from support: cane wigwams, fan trellises, and wires in the greenhouse are all effective. Cucurbits are pollinated by insects (except greenhouse cucumbers, which are all-female and do not need pollinating). Female flowers can be hand-pollinated if necessary. Powdery mildew may occur, and cucumber mosaic virus can cause deformed fruits; grow resistant varieties if possible. Red spider mites and whiteflies can be a problem on greenhouse crops.

Harvest and storage Leave pumpkins and squashes on the plant until they have a hard skin and cracked stem, and for longer, if possible, if they are to be stored. Cut with a long stem and cure in a warm room for several days, before storing somewhere cooler.

Sowing depths and spacing

CROP	SOWING DEPTH	SPACING (PLANTS)
Cucumbers	1 in (2.5 cm)	30 in (75 cm)
Pumpkin/winter squash	1 in (2.5 cm)	3–6 ft (90 cm–1.8 m)
Zucchini/summer squash	1 in (2.5 cm)	3–4 ft (90 cm–1.2 m)

Pumpkins do not tolerate frost and must be harvested before temperatures fall below freezing.

Cultivation tips

Male and female flowers Some cucurbits may need hand pollination: female flowers have mini-fruits behind them (*above*), while male flowers grow on a thin stem. Remove male cucumber flowers in the greenhouse to prevent pollination and deformed, bitter fruits.

Training squashes Raise trailing squash plants off the ground to make them tidier and stop the fruit from rotting on damp soil and being eaten by slugs. Anchor canes in the ground at an angle, linking them together with strong twine and attaching them to a fence.

Crops to choose

Zucchini Easy to grow and productive, zucchini usually has a bush, rather than trailing, habit, and suits small gardens.

Cucumber The smooth-skinned greenhouse types of cucumbers are more difficult to grow than outdoor ridge varieties.

Summer squash Strangely shaped, soft-skinned squashes taste the same as zucchini and can be cooked in the same way.

Pumpkin A late summer bounty in the garden. Select varieties grown for flavor rather than size if they are for the kitchen.

Fruiting vegetables

These sun-loving crops are a popular choice for patio containers and warm windowsills. There are varieties to suit every size of garden and all kinds of climate, and the right selection will yield delicious late summer crops.

How to grow

Site and soil Provide a warm, sunny site, with light, fertile, well-drained soil for these tender crops. All, except sweet corn, will flourish in containers, in a greenhouse or by a sunny wall. Warm the soil by covering with cloches or clear plastic before planting.

Sowing and planting out Sow crops under cover, at 60°F (16°C) or warmer, in early spring. Where small numbers are required, sow seeds into individual pots of multipurpose potting mix, and cover with sifted potting mix. Keep growing seedlings in a well-lit place. Harden plants off in a cold frame or outside under fleece for a week before erecting supports and planting out in the final positions. Pots should be at least 10 in (25 cm) wide and deep, or you can use growing bags. Sweet corn can be direct-sown outdoors in mild areas from mid-spring.

Care and potential problems Water well during flowering and when fruits are developing. Cordon tomatoes need tying into supports, and sideshoots that appear where leaves join the main stem should be pinched out. Pinch out the growing tips of eggplants and peppers to encourage compact growth. When fruits begin to set, apply a liquid fertilizer weekly. Aphids, red spider mites, and whiteflies are common on crops grown under cover, as is botrytis (gray mold). Tomatoes are susceptible to blight, potato cyst eelworm, and viruses. Sweet corn is a favorite with animal pests; mice eat seed in the soil, while birds, squirrels, and raccoons can ruin crops.

Harvest and storage Pick eggplants while the skin is glossy. Uproot outdoor tomatoes and peppers before the first frost and hang in a greenhouse to ripen the last fruits. Check sweet corn for maturity when the silks turn brown by piercing a kernel; white juice shows ripeness.

A truss of tomatoes, ripe for harvesting.

Sowing depths and spacing

CROP	SOWING DEPTH	SPACING	
		Plants	Rows
Eggplants	½ in (1 cm)	18 in (45 cm)	24 in (60 cm)
Peppers (sweet and hot)	½ in (1 cm)	18 in (45 cm)	24 in (60 cm)
Tomatoes, bush	¾ in (2 cm)	24 in (60 cm)	24 in (60 cm)
cordon	¾ in (2 cm)	18 in (45 cm)	24 in (60 cm)
Sweet corn	1½ in (4 cm)	18 in (45 cm)	18 in (45 cm)

Cultivation tips

Watering tomatoes The best way to water tomatoes is to insert a pot, or a plastic bottle cut in half, with holes in the base, into the soil next to each tomato plant and water into it. This delivers moisture directly to the deeper roots and reduces evaporation rates.

Assisting sweet corn fertilization Arrange plants in dense blocks where the pollen will be concentrated, to maximize the yield. These plants rely on the wind to disperse their pollen, and planting in this way encourages the best possible crop.

Crops to choose

Sweet corn These plants look stately in flower beds, and the freshly picked cobs, cooked seconds after harvest, taste terrific.

Sweet pepper Easy to grow, the long, thin-walled varieties of grilling pepper look pretty on the plant and have good flavor.

Eggplant When pinched out to keep them bushy, eggplants make attractive plants for patio pots in warm areas.

Chili pepper Easy to grow, these fiery fruits only ripen reliably under cover. Try them on a windowsill and freeze any excess.

Perennial and stem vegetables

Often disappointing when store-bought, these vegetables are a gourmet treat when freshly picked. They are easy to grow, and perennial types also suit the ornamental garden. The stem vegetables celery and celeriac are not perennials.

Apply fertilizer to asparagus in early spring.

How to grow

Site and soil Choose a sunny, open site, with deep, free-draining soil, and fork in plenty of organic matter before planting. Celery thrives only in very rich, moist soil, so if your soil is poor, you may do better with celeriac.

Sowing and planting out Asparagus and globe artichokes are difficult to grow from seed, so many gardeners start in spring with asparagus crowns and young globe artichoke plants. To plant asparagus, dig a trench 8 in (20 cm) deep and at the bottom make a central ridge with soil; spread the crown's roots over the ridge and cover with soil so that just the tips are showing. Plant globe artichokes in rows, keeping the leaf rosette above the soil. Simply bury Jerusalem artichoke tubers in the soil. Sow celery and celeriac seed indoors from mid-spring and harden off when they have five to six leaves, before planting out. Water plants in well. Self-blanching celery is an easy choice for beginners.

Care and potential problems Jerusalem artichokes may need support. Water and mulch globe artichokes in dry weather. Mulch the asparagus bed with organic matter, and apply fertilizer in early spring and after harvesting. Cut down when growth yellows in fall. Water celery and celeriac weekly, and mulch with straw or compost. Globe artichokes may be attacked by black bean aphids, and Jerusalem types can be invasive, so keep them in check. Fungal rots may affect all crops in wet weather.

Harvest and storage Harvest celery plants whole before the first frost. Celeriac is hardy and best left in the ground until required. Cut asparagus spears about 2 in (5 cm) below the soil surface when they are about 6 in (15 cm) tall. Cut the heads of globe artichokes while still tight. Unearth Jerusalem artichokes as and when required.

Sowing depths and spacing

CROP	SOWING DEPTH	SPACING	
		Plants	Rows
Celery	On surface	10 in (25 cm)	10 in (25 cm)
Celeriac	On surface	12 in (30 cm)	12 in (30 cm)
Asparagus	1 in (2.5 cm)	10 in (25 cm)	12 in (30 cm)
Globe artichoke	n/a	30 in (75 cm)	36 in (90 cm)
Jerusalem artichoke	4 in (10 cm)	12 in (30 cm)	12 in (30 cm)

Cultivation tips

Earthing up celery Trench celery is a traditional garden crop (*see left*). The stems are blanched by covering the stems with soil, known as "earthing up," to exclude light. Tie the stems together with string when the plant is 12 in (30 cm) tall, and pile soil around them to half their height. Repeat every three weeks until just the tops are showing in late fall.

Mulching globe artichokes Globe artichokes, particularly young plants and those growing in cold areas, can be damaged by frost, so protect them during the winter by earthing up around them and covering the plant with a 6-in- (15-cm-) thick mulch of straw, or a double layer of horticultural fleece.

Harvesting young asparagus plants Patience is a virtue when establishing an asparagus bed. Resist harvesting the spears for the first two years after planting, to allow the plants to gather strength for future years. Harvest for six weeks in late spring in the third year and for eight weeks in the years that follow.

Crops to choose

Celery Self-blanching varieties are best grown close together in tight blocks or cold frames to produce tender, pale stems.

Celeriac This knobby vegetable tastes much better than it looks and is delicious roasted, mashed, or in soups.

Globe artichoke A tall, easy-to-grow decorative plant with silvery foliage. The mature flower buds are a real delicacy.

Jerusalem artichoke The tubers are usually cooked but can be eaten raw. Plants are tall and make a good windbreak.

Salad and leafy vegetables and herbs

Everyone has room for a little pot of herbs or a window box of cut-and-come-again salad leaves. They are so easy to grow that you'll wonder how you managed before without all those fresh flavors on your doorstep.

How to grow

Site and soil Salad crops, chard, and many herbs tolerate most soils, except waterlogged, and don't demand a lot of soil preparation. However, spinach and Asian greens need rich, fertile, nonacidic soil. All do well in containers and full sun, but lettuces need shade in high summer.

Sowing and planting out Leafy salads germinate quickly in warm conditions, but avoid extremes of heat or cold. Sow salads in modules under cover from early spring; sow spinach, Swiss chard, and bok choy outdoors in light shade. Successional sowings of small numbers of seeds help to guarantee a continuous supply of leaves. Plant out module-grown seedlings when their roots have filled the container, and water well. Thin directly sown seedlings to the appropriate spacing.
  Tender herbs, such as basil, are often grown from seed; hardy herbs are usually bought as young plants. Sow seeds under cover in early spring; plant out after the last frost.

Care and potential problems Keep rows of salads and leafy crops weed-free and don't let them dry out, to discourage bolting. Protect early or late crops from frost with cloches or fleece. Trim herbs regularly to keep them tidy and productive; water those in containers frequently.
  Slugs and snails, as well as clubroot and caterpillars on brassicas, are the biggest problems. Lettuces are prone to fungal rots in wet weather; mildew can spoil spinach crops.

Harvest and storage Leafy salads are best eaten fresh. Cut hearting lettuces and bok choy at their base; pick leaves as needed from loose-leaf lettuces, cut-and-come-again crops, spinach, and chard. Use herbs fresh, or dry or freeze them.

Sowing depths and spacing

CROP	SOWING DEPTH	SPACING	
		Plants	Rows
Lettuce	½ in (1 cm)	6–12 in (15–30 cm)	6–12 in (15–30 cm)
Mizuna/mibuna	½ in (1 cm)	4–6 in (10–15 cm)	6 in (15 cm)
Arugula	½ in (1 cm)	6 in (15 cm)	6 in (15 cm)
Spinach	1 in (2.5 cm)	3–6 in (8–15 cm)	12 in (30 cm)
Chard	1 in (2.5 cm)	8 in (20 cm)	18 in (45 cm)
Basil	¼ in (0.5 cm)	8 in (20 cm)	8 in (20 cm)
Parsley	¼ in (0.5 cm)	8 in (20 cm)	12 in (30 cm)
Cilantro	¼ in (0.5 cm)	8 in (20 cm)	12 in (30 cm)

Colorful red-leaved lettuce 'Great Dixter'.

Cultivation tips

Preventing lettuce and spinach from bolting In hot weather and when the soil is dry, lettuces, spinach, and many other leafy crops bolt, which is when plants go to seed and leaves become bitter (*see left*). Prevent or delay this by keeping the soil moist with regular watering and by planting summer crops in light shade rather than full sun.

Halting the spread of mint With its underground runners, mint can become an invasive nuisance in the garden, so it is best to grow it in a container or at least in a pot sunk into the soil. The latter will help to prevent it from taking over, but may not confine it forever.

Propagating perennial herbs Renew the vigor of old woody perennial herbs by digging them up in late summer and dividing them. Using pruners, cut the plants into small sections with plenty of healthy roots and leaves, which you can then replant. This works particularly well for thyme, chives, and oregano, but division is not suitable for shrubby herbs, such as sage and rosemary.

Crops to choose

Spinach A very nutritious crop and easy to grow. Harvest baby leaves to use in salads, or mature leaves for steaming.

Swiss chard This striking crop is grown for its colored stems, which look good on the plate, and can be steamed or eaten fresh.

Apple mint Furry, with a mild, sweet flavor, this is the best mint for flavoring vegetables and to stroke as you walk past.

Purple sage This bushy, purple-tinged plant is so attractive that it is often planted in flowerbeds. It tastes good, too.

How to grow vegetables

Success in the vegetable garden
is not difficult to achieve, especially
if you master the basic techniques
outlined in this chapter. These help
to ensure that your crops get off to
a flying start, and that they remain
healthy and productive. There is also
advice on making the most of small
spaces by combining fast- and slow-
growing vegetables, and tips on
harvesting and storing your produce.

Sowing beet seeds outside

When sowing outdoors, the soil must be warm enough in spring for seeds to germinate (wait for the first weed seeds to sprout if you are unsure). Choose a dry day when the soil is moist to rake it to a fine, crumbly texture (tilth) for sowing.

Tip for success

For easy sowing, buy seeds that are attached at intervals to a biodegradable tape, which can simply be laid in the drill.

1 For a straight row, pull a string line tight across the seed bed and make a V-shaped drill by dragging the corner of a hoe along the string. Make the drill about 1 in (2.5 cm) deep for beet seeds (the depth varies for different crops).

2 Pour seeds into the palm of your hand and sow them one at a time at 2-in (5-cm) intervals along the row. (Spacings vary for different seeds according to their size; tiny seeds should be sown as thinly and evenly as possible.)

3 As soon as sowing is complete, use the back of a rake to push the soil gently over the drill. Mark the row clearly with a plant label so you know what you have sown where, and don't disturb the germinating seeds.

4 Keep rows free of weeds. Remove excess seedlings by pulling them out with their roots, or pinching them off at soil level when they are large enough to handle. This ensures that the remaining plants have enough space.

Sowing red cabbage seeds for transplanting

Sowing under cover is the best way to give plants a head start. They can then be planted out after the risk of frost has passed. If you don't have a heated greenhouse, simply place your seed trays on a warm windowsill.

1 Fill a seed tray with seed-starting mix, and gently firm with a board or second tray to eliminate air pockets. Using a watering can with a fine spray, water the soil lightly and allow to drain before sowing.

2 Distribute the seeds evenly over the surface of the moist soil by scattering them from their packet or from your hand. Sow the seeds thinly to prevent overcrowding once they have germinated.

3 Use a garden sieve to cover the seeds with a thin layer of fine-grade, lump-free seed-starting mix, then very gently firm it over the seeds with the palm of your hand.

4 Lightly water the soil using a watering can with a fine spray, or stand the tray in water until the surface darkens, then allow to drain. Label the tray to help you keep track of what you have sown.

Sowing red cabbage seeds for transplanting *continued*

5 Provide warm, humid conditions by placing the tray in a propagator or covering it with glass or plastic. As soon as seedlings emerge, remove the cover, but protect them from strong sunlight. Turn trays on windowsills regularly.

6 When the first seed leaves are fully developed, prick the seedlings out. Fill a module tray with moist potting mix. Water the seedlings and, holding each by a leaf, loosen the soil with a pencil or dibber and tease its roots free.

7 Dibble a hole in every module and carefully lower a seedling into each, using the dibber to firm the soil around the roots. Water them in and label the tray. Grow the seedlings on until they have filled their new containers.

8 When the weather is warmer, place the young plants outside in a closed cold frame. To give them a chance to harden off (acclimatize), gradually increase the ventilation over two weeks, until they are uncovered.

9 Plant out hardened-off plants in their final position in already prepared soil. Red cabbages should be 12 in (30 cm) apart with 18 in (45 cm) between rows. If pigeons are a problem, protect plants with netting.

Growing zucchini from plug plants

If space and time for growing vegetables from seed are tight, buy plug plants at garden centers or by mail order. They are more expensive than seed and the choice of varieties is limited, but they do offer an easy way to get started.

1 Buy compact, green plants with a healthy root system. Water well and plant out or pot on immediately to avoid checking their growth. Beware of buying zucchini and other half-hardy plants before the risk of frost has passed.

2 Carefully remove each seedling from its packaging and, holding the root ball rather than the delicate leaves, plant them into prepared soil so that the top of the root ball is just below soil level.

3 Gently firm the soil around each plant so that it is stable and water well to help it get established. Add a mulch of organic material around each plant (but not touching the stem) to retain soil moisture and suppress weeds.

4 Label, and add supports for plants that need them as they grow. Cloches are often useful to protect young plants from cold and windy weather. Continue to water the plants regularly until they are established.

Growing first early potatoes

Potatoes are easy to grow and usually ready to harvest after they have flowered. At 10–12 weeks, pull some soil aside to check if tubers are ready and lift the roots carefully with a fork.

Tip for success

Potatoes do well in large pots. Plant chitted tubers in a pot half-full of potting mix. When shoots emerge, add more mix to fill.

1 In late winter, place your seed potatoes in egg cartons or trays with the maximum number of buds (eyes) pointing upward. Stand the boxes in a cool, light place indoors for about six weeks to produce sturdy, dark sprouts (chitting).

2 When shoots reach about 1 in (2.5 cm) long, in early spring, mark a row in prepared soil. At 12-in (30-cm) intervals, dig holes about 4 in (10 cm) deep and plant a single tuber in each, with its shoots pointing upward.

3 Fill each hole with soil, rake over the row, and mark its position. A general-purpose fertilizer can also be applied at the specified rate on either side of the row at this stage, or it may be worked into the soil before planting.

4 Tubers exposed to light will turn green, making them toxic and inedible. To avoid this, earth up the plants as they emerge by mounding soil around their stems to a height of around 6 in (15 cm).

Growing runner beans

Runner beans grow best in rich, fertile soil, so prepare your site by digging in plenty of organic matter at least two weeks before planting. Plant scented flowers, such as sweet peas, nearby to attract pollinating insects to the garden.

1   Support is vital for these climbing plants. Build a wigwam from eight canes, ideally at least 7 ft (2.2 m) long, pushed firmly into the soil about 12 in (30 cm) apart, in a circle. Tie the canes securely at the top and again halfway down.

2   From late spring, when the soil is at least 54°F (12°C), plant two seeds at a depth of 2 in (5 cm) by each cane and water thoroughly. In cold areas or where the soil is heavy, sow the seeds in deep pots indoors in mid-spring.

3   After germination, remove the weaker seedling. Twist the remaining plant around its cane and tie it in with twine. A companion sweet pea plant will attract insects to the runner bean flowers, promoting a good crop.

4   It is important to pick runner beans regularly (at least twice a week), when they are young and tender, because overly mature pods are less appetizing and suppress the formation of new flowers.

Planting tomatoes in a growing bag

Growing bags dry out rapidly, but the volume of potting mix can be increased, and the need to water reduced, by planting into open-ended pots inserted into holes in the bag, as shown here.

Tip for success

Other summer crops, such as lettuce, suit growing bags, taking only 8–12 weeks from seed to the cropping stage.

1 Using a knife, carefully cut three openings in the top of the growing bag and cut drainage holes in the base. If using bottomless pots (buy ready-made, or make your own), insert them into the openings and fill with soil.

2 When the plants are hardened off and the first flowers are about to open, plant into the bag or the pots so that the top of the root ball is just below the soil surface. Firm the soil around the roots and water well.

3 Add canes or strong wires for support. Take care to pinch out all fast-growing sideshoots between the leaves and stem—they divert valuable energy away from fruit production. Apply a liquid tomato fertilizer weekly.

4 Tie in the main stems with twine as they grow. Stop the plant from growing taller by removing the growing tip, two leaves beyond the fifth or sixth cluster (truss) of fruit. This diverts the plant's energy into the last fruits of the season.

Growing chard in a container

A large pot filled with the glossy green leaves and neon-colored stems of chard 'Bright Lights' will add color to any patio. Harvest the baby leaves for salads when young, or allow them to mature for steaming and stir-frying.

Tip for success

Test different layouts in your container while the plants are still in their own pots to help create the best color display.

1 Position the empty pot in a sunny, sheltered spot. Ensure that the container has drainage holes, cover the base with a layer of crocks, and add multipurpose potting mix to within about 1 in (2.5 cm) of the container's lip.

2 Water the young chard plants and carefully remove them from their pots, holding them by the roots rather than leaves. Gently tease out the roots to help them establish quickly and space them about 4 in (10 cm) apart.

3 Place the plants into holes made in the potting mix at the correct spacing, checking that the top of the root ball is just below soil level. Gently firm soil around each plant and water the container thoroughly.

4 Water the chard regularly to keep the large leaves firm and in good condition, especially during hot summer weather. You can also apply a nitrogen-rich fertilizer to help maintain vigorous healthy growth.

Sprouting seeds

Many kinds of beans and seeds are available for sprouting, providing a range of interesting flavors and textures. All sprouting seeds will grow in jars or tiered sprouters, which allow several crops to be grown at once.

1 Thoroughly clean the container before each use. Pour seeds into a sprouting jar (with a mesh lid for easy draining), fill it with cold water, and leave the seeds to soak for 8–12 hours. Do not overfill the jar.

2 Once the seeds have soaked, invert the jar over a sink, then rinse the seeds with cold water and drain again, making sure that they are not standing in water. Place the jar out of direct sunlight, where air circulation is good.

3 Rinse and drain the seeds with cold water twice a day to keep them clean and moist. Alfalfa seeds sprout after only 2 days and are ready to eat 2–4 days after that. Try a few as the shoots lengthen to find your favorite eating stage.

4 When they are ready, give the sprouts a final rinse, drain, and leave for 8 hours to allow excess water to evaporate. The sprouts can then be stored in the refrigerator for up to 5 days. Discard the crop if mold develops.

Intercropping lettuce and corn

Planting a slow-growing and a fast-maturing crop together in a grid pattern is an efficient way to make the most of limited space. Lettuces can be grown among sweet corn plants and picked before the cobs mature.

1 Measure and mark out a grid of 18-in (45-cm) squares. Use bamboo canes to mark the lines in the soil. This block arrangement is also ideal for maximizing the wind pollination of sweet corn.

2 Transplant one young corn plant in the corner of each square. Firm the soil around the base of each plant. (Corn plants are tender, so they may have to be raised from seed under cover, *see pp.60–63*.)

3 Mix the lettuce seed with fine sand and scatter thinly in between the corn plants. Rake over carefully. The lettuces will mature in 8–12 weeks and fill the gaps in between the corn plants.

4 Thin the lettuce seedlings to 3–4 plants per square. Sweet corn takes at least 16 weeks to produce mature cobs, but the lettuce can be harvested long before the corn casts too much shade on them.

Planting an herb garden

This formal herb feature takes only a day to build and a season to mature. Here, bricks have been used to edge the beds and divide them into quarters. A potted bay tree forms the centerpiece.

1 Mark out a cross with pegs and string. Dig trenches following the string lines, just wider and not quite as deep as the bricks to allow space for the bricks to settle. Use a hammer handle to firm in the bricks.

2 Finish the last quarter and bed the bricks down securely, packing the soil firmly against them (no need to mortar them in). If you wish to have a plant in the center of the feature, make sure you leave space for it.

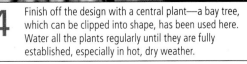

3 Arrange the plants in their pots before they go in the ground, so you can adjust the spacing if required. Water each plant thoroughly before removing it from its pot. Make planting holes and insert the plants. Water well.

4 Finish off the design with a central plant—a bay tree, which can be clipped into shape, has been used here. Water all the plants regularly until they are fully established, especially in hot, dry weather.

Herbs in painted pots

Pots are ideal for herbs—they enjoy the constricted space and can be clipped to size. Painting simple clay pots with complementary colors and mulching with slate adds to the appeal.

1 Rub down and clean the surface of a 1-quart (1-liter) clay pot. Paint each one with either flat latex or exterior gloss paint, depending on the effect you want to achieve.

2 Break up polystyrene packaging that bedding plants are sold in to form a layer of crocks at the bottom of the pot. Polystyrene is light, easily broken, and can be used instead of terra-cotta. Add some multipurpose potting mix.

3 Position the plant to check that it will be planted at the same depth as in its original container. Water it, and then remove it from its pot. If it is root-bound, tease out the roots to encourage it to establish.

4 Position the herb in the pot. Fill in with soil around the plant and firm it in. Water the pot well and cover the soil surface with small slate chips. These act as a good water conserver and decorative feature.

Constructing a raised bed

Raised beds make good use of space and are an efficient way of growing crops. The soil drains well, warms up rapidly in spring, and can be tended from the path, avoiding soil compaction.

Tip for success

Make sure the soil is level by stretching a length of string across the raised bed. Bricks will keep the string taut.

1 Decide on the bed size. The ideal width is 4 ft (1.2 m), to allow easy cultivation from the path, but beds can be any length. Cut four edging boards to the correct length and nail on wooden pegs about 4 in (10 cm) from the ends.

2 Lay out the boards in their final positions and drive the wooden pegs into the soil with a mallet. Check that each timber is straight using a level, making adjustments by pounding the higher end down with a mallet.

3 Rest a piece of wood diagonally across two edging timbers, place a level on it, and make any necessary adjustments. Before building another bed, ensure that you leave a path wide enough for easy access.

4 Fill the bed with good-quality topsoil that has been improved with organic matter, such as garden compost or well-rotted manure. Spread the soil evenly and level the surface with the back of a rake. Top off as the soil settles.

Harvesting and storing

Picking fresh produce is always rewarding, and the taste of home-grown vegetables cannot be beaten, but it is important to harvest crops correctly to prevent damage. This way, waste is minimized and productivity continues.

Fresh produce Many crops are at their tastiest when small and tender, and eaten just minutes after picking. It is a good idea to walk around the garden every day in summer, harvesting what looks good, in order to avoid giant zucchini, stringy beans, and bolted lettuces.

Pulling beets Lift beets as required once they have reached about 2 in (5 cm) in diameter. Simply take a firm hold of the stems and pull the root from the soil. Lift alternate roots in a row to leave more space for the others.

Cutting asparagus Cut tender spears 1 in (2.5 cm) below soil level every 2–5 days over a period of 8 weeks in mid-spring. Curved, serrated asparagus knives are specially designed for this purpose.

Lifting potatoes Once the plants have flowered, gently pull aside the soil and turn it over with a fork, picking up potatoes as you go. Dig about 12 in (30 cm) from the stem to prevent the tubers from being damaged.

Picking corn Test cobs for ripeness as soon as the tassels turn brown: pull back the protective leaves; when ready, sap from the cut kernels will be milky. Then hold the stem firmly and twist the cob to break it off.

Harvesting and storing *continued*

Drying and curing

A number of crops will store well only if they have been allowed to ripen fully and then left to dry in a warm, well-ventilated place. This is true of onions, shallots, garlic, and dried beans, along with pumpkins and winter squashes. The following are simple methods, but they must be carefully observed to prevent the stored crop from rotting or spoiling.

Curing pumpkins and squashes Leave the fruits on the plant until they are fully colored and sound a hollow note when tapped. Cut them from the plant with a sharp knife, leaving the longest stem possible, and allow the skins to harden, or cure, in the sun, a greenhouse, or a warm room for several days. Pumpkins will keep until spring in a cool, slightly humid room, where they can also be used as decoration.

Drying onions and beans Let the foliage of onions, shallots, and garlic die down naturally before lifting with a fork and laying them out to dry in the sun on a wire rack. Once the bulbs are dry, brush off any loose skins and soil, and hang them in bunches or nets in a cool, light place. Beans to be stored dry should be allowed to mature on the plant and harvested before the pods split. Lay the pods on a wire rack and allow them to dry in a cool place, after which you can shell the beans. Allow the beans to dry again before putting them in jars and storing in a cool, dark place.

Pumpkins and squashes are ornamental as well as a useful crop.

Spread out borlotti beans on wire mesh to dry in the sun.

Harvest shallots and dry on a wire rack in the sun.

Storing potatoes

Lift maincrop potatoes on a dry day. Allow them to dry on the ground for a few hours, then select undamaged tubers for storage. A double-layered paper sack, kept in a cool, dry place such as a garage or basement, is usually the most practical way of storing them. Potatoes must be kept in the dark to keep them from turning green, so close the sack tightly. Wooden boxes can also be used, but plastic containers are unsuitable, because they retain moisture, making tubers susceptible to rot.

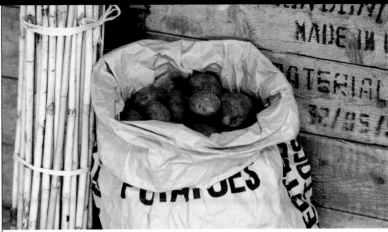
Potatoes store well in a cool, dry place, as long as they are kept in the dark.

Storing roots

Most roots, except turnips and beets, can be left in the ground until required, even over winter. However, after lifting, root crops also store well in a cool, dry place. Arrange undamaged roots in a shallow wooden box so they are not touching, and cover with moist sand. Roots can also be stored against a wall outdoors in a "clamp," where roots are stacked on a layer of sand and covered with a layer of straw and then soil. This protects them from frost, but rodents can be a problem.

Parsnips store well in moist sand.

A "clamp" protects rutabagas from frost.

Freezing and preserving

One of the best ways to deal with gluts of many vegetables is to freeze them. This can also be a useful way of storing summer herbs for winter. Fennel, basil, and parsley all freeze well when cleaned and put in labeled bags. Chopped herbs can also be conveniently frozen with a little water in ice cube trays. Alternatively, add a sprig of herbs and perhaps a chili pepper to a bottle of olive oil, to infuse it with fresh summer flavors.

Herbs freeze well.

Herbs and chili pepper add flavor to olive oil.

Planting recipes

Vegetables can be grown in a variety of imaginative ways, and the recipes here show how to make the best use of containers, vertical spaces, and ornamental gardens. The symbols below are used to indicate the conditions each plant prefers.

Key to plant symbols

Soil preference

◊ Well-drained soil

◖ Moist soil

◆ Wet soil

Preference for sun or shade

☼ Full sun

☼ Partial or dappled shade

☀ Full shade

Hardiness ratings

✳✳✳ Fully hardy plants

✳✳ Plants that survive outside in mild regions or sheltered sites

✳ Plants that need protection from frost over winter

✿ Tender plants that do not tolerate any degree of frost

Vertical vegetable garden

Vertical space is often underused, but it has great potential in small gardens, increasing the space for growing a range of crops. Attaching pots of herbs and bush varieties of vegetables to a sturdy wire mesh can turn a bare sunny wall into a riot of color, and they are simple to care for and convenient to harvest. Vigorous climbing beans, squashes, and nasturtiums can be planted in large containers at the base of the wall and are easy to train up the mesh for a fabulous, lush display.

Garden basics

Size 6 x 7 ft (1.8 x 2.2 m)

Suits Any sunny location with a wall or fence as a backdrop

Soil Light, multipurpose potting mix

Site Wall in full sun

Shopping list

- 2 x eggplant 'Mohican'
- 3 x basil 'Sweet Genovese'
- 3 x basil 'Red Rubin'
- 3 x tomato 'Tumbling Tom Red'
- 1 x cucumber 'Masterpiece'
- 1 x zucchini 'Tromboncino'
- 3 x runner bean 'Wisley Magic'

Planting and aftercare

Attach wood battens to the wall and secure a sturdy wire mesh to them. Drill holes in the sides of plastic pots and window boxes and thread galvanized wire through them before planting. After the risk of frost has passed, fill the pots with a lightweight potting mix, plant with hardened-off plants, secure pots to the mesh, and arrange larger ones at the base of the wall. Leave space for plants to develop, and train climbing crops up the mesh. Water the plants frequently because they will dry out rapidly in their exposed position. Tie in climbing plants as they grow and harvest frequently to encourage further crops.

Eggplant 'Mohican'

Basil 'Sweet Genovese', 'Red Rubin'

Tomato 'Tumbling Tom Red'

Cucumber 'Masterpiece'

Zucchini 'Tromboncino'

Runner bean 'Wisley Magic'

Hanging herb and vegetable basket

Vegetable gardening does not get much more convenient than picking juicy cherry tomatoes and fragrant herbs from just outside your back door. Hanging baskets are often associated with bedding plants, but why not try planting a combination of cascading cherry tomatoes, vibrant nasturtiums, and delicious herbs instead? Kept fertilized and watered, they will look great over a long season and provide tasty fresh produce for the kitchen as well.

Container basics

Size Basket at least 10 in (25 cm) in diameter

Suits Area close to the kitchen

Soil Multipurpose potting mix

Site Wall in full sun and sheltered from strong winds

Shopping list

- 1 x chocolate peppermint 'Chocolate'
- 1 x parsley 'Forest Green'
- 1 x lemon thyme 'Golden Lemon'
- 1 x tomato 'Tumbler'
- 1 x chives
- 1 x nasturtium 'African Queen'

Planting and aftercare

Ensure that drainage holes have been made in the base of the basket. Place a layer of lightweight potting mix in the bottom of the basket, then position the plants, still in their pots, to see where they will look best. Remember that trailing plants should be near the edge. Once you have settled on a design, water the plants well, remove them from their pots, and place in the basket. Fill the gaps with potting mix, firming around the plants, and water the basket thoroughly. Hang it on a sturdy hook and water regularly. Once tomatoes begin to set, apply a liquid tomato fertilizer weekly.

Peppermint 'Chocolate'

Parsley 'Forest Green'

Lemon thyme 'Golden Lemon'

Tomato 'Tumbler'

Chives

Nasturtium 'African Queen'

Cut-and-come-again window box

Even without a garden, it is possible to grow a good supply of tasty baby salad leaves. Cut-and-come-again salads are one of the quickest and easiest crops to grow from seed and, when grown in a window box, could not be more convenient to care for and harvest. Try growing your own mix of lettuce, Asian greens, and arugula to create a peppery salad, which tastes wonderfully fresh when it has gone from plant to plate in a matter of seconds.

Window box basics

Size 20 x 6 in (50 x 15 cm)

Suits Window sill where a window box can be secured

Soil Good, multipurpose potting mix

Site Window sill with access for watering, in full sun or partial shade

Shopping list

- 1 x packet mibuna seeds
- 1 x packet mizuna seeds
- 1 x packet lettuce 'Oakleaf' or 'Salad Bowl Mixed' seeds
- 1 x packet arugula seeds

Planting and aftercare

Choose a window sill in sun or partial shade, which can be reached easily for watering and harvesting. Make sure the window box is secured and has drainage holes in the base. Add a layer of crocks to the box and fill it to within ¾ in (2 cm) of the top with multipurpose potting mix. Blend the different seeds together in a bowl and sow thinly from the palm of your hand from mid-spring until late summer. Cover with a thin layer of potting mix and water well. Germination is rapid and the first leaves can be cut with scissors after 3–5 weeks, leaving a 2-in (5-cm) stump to regrow. Two or three further harvests can be cut at 3–5-week intervals. Water the window box regularly for a healthy crop.

Mibuna

Mizuna

Lettuce 'Oakleaf'

Additional plant idea

Arugula 'Rocket Wild'

Decorative climbing display

Few flower and vegetable combinations could be more eye-catching than this mix of exotic purple blooms and bulging orange squashes. The vigorous growth of squashes is perfect for training up a fence and provides an interesting contrast to the delicate foliage of the climbing passion flower and cup-and-saucer plants. All of these plants flourish in summer heat, so will perform best in warmer areas with a long growing season.

Border basics

Size 6 x 6 ft (2 x 2 m)

Suits Vegetable or ornamental garden with a fence or trellis as a backdrop

Soil Fertile, moist, but well-drained

Site Border in front of fence or trellis in full sun

Shopping list

- 1 x squash 'Uchiki Kuri' or 'Jack Be Little'
- 1 x passion flower (*Passiflora caerulea*)
- 1 x cup-and-saucer plant (*Cobaea scandens*)

Planting and aftercare

Sow squash and cup-and-saucer plant seeds under cover in mid-spring, in either a warm room or a heated propagator. Passion flowers are readily available as plants and will persist as perennial climbers in warm gardens. Attach wires or trellis to a bare fence, so the climbing plants can be tied in or use their own tendrils for support.

After the last frost date, plant the young plants about 12 in (30 cm) away from the base of the fence, about 18 in (45 cm) apart, and water them well. Tie the stems to the supports when they are long enough, after which the passion flower and cup-and-saucer plant should find their own way, while the squash may need further tying in. Water the squashes regularly once fruits have formed.

Squash 'Uchiki Kuri'

Passion flower (*Passiflora*)

Cup-and-saucer plant (*Cobaea*)

Alternative squash

Squash 'Jack Be Little'

Exotic vegetable raised bed

If you have a sheltered, sunny wall that absorbs the sun's heat during the day and warms the surrounding air at night, take advantage of this microclimate to grow exotic crops. This raised bed has been filled with heat-loving tomatoes, peppers, eggplants, and feathery-leaved garbanzo (chickpea) plants, as well as cucumbers and sweet potatoes that scramble up the wall. Some of these vegetables only crop well in hot summers, but they make attractive curiosities that are fun to try.

Eggplant 'Moneymaker'

Cucumber 'Carmen'

Border basics

Size 6 x 3 ft (2 x 1 m)

Suits Any style of garden

Soil Fertile, moist, but free-draining

Site Border in front of a wall in full sun, in warm regions

Shopping list

- 1 x eggplant 'Moneymaker'
- 1 x cucumber 'Carmen'
- 1 x sweet pepper 'Gypsy'
- 1 x tomato 'Summer Sweet'
- 1 x garbanzo 'Principe'
- 1 x sweet potato 'Beauregard'

Planting and aftercare

Sow seeds of tomatoes, cucumbers, sweet peppers, and eggplants under cover in spring. Once the risk of frost has passed, harden the young plants off and plant them out in the raised bed. It is a good idea to soak the garbanzos in regularly changed water for a few days until they sprout before planting them in their final positions. Plant the sweet potato "slips" with about 2 in (5 cm) of stem above the soil and, as with the other young plants, water well. Attach wire mesh to the wall and train the cucumber and sweet potato stems through it. Once the first fruits have set, fertilize weekly with a tomato fertilizer that is high in potash. Crops should be ready to harvest in late summer.

Sweet pepper 'Gypsy'

Tomato 'Summer Sweet'

Garbanzo 'Principe'

Sweet potato 'Beauregard'

Courtyard vegetable garden

Even a modest corner of the garden can be enough to grow an interesting range of vegetables that will crop well over a long season. Here, cordon tomatoes and runner beans have been trained up the wall and fence to make the best use of the vertical space. Edging the path is a densely sown crop of cut-and-come-again lettuce. Red cabbage and sweet corn will extend the harvest into late summer and early fall, the zucchini in the pot until mid-fall.

Border basics

Size 12 x 6 ft (4 x 2 m)

Suits Courtyard garden

Soil Fertile, moist, but free-draining

Site Corner of garden, sheltered by a wall or fence, in full sun

Shopping list

- 3 x tomato 'Gardener's Delight'
- 3 x runner bean 'Liberty'
- 1 x zucchini 'Burpee's Golden'
- 9 x sweet corn 'Swift'
- 1 x packet lettuce seed 'Salad Bowl Mixed'
- 3 x cabbage 'Marner Early Red'

Planting and aftercare

Prepare the area by digging in plenty of organic matter, ideally in fall. Buy plug plants or, where there is space under cover, sow tomato, runner bean, red cabbage, and sweet corn seeds in pots, harden them off, and plant out after the risk of frost has passed. Plant tomatoes in a growing bag because they thrive on the rich soil, adding canes for support and pinching out sideshoots as they grow. Give the runner beans wires to climb up. Plant sweet corn in a block to aid pollination, and direct-sow a few lettuce seeds regularly to ensure a continuous crop. Water young plants in, and continue watering and fertilizing regularly those in growing bags.

Tomato 'Gardener's Delight'

Runner bean 'Liberty'

Zucchini 'Burpee's Golden'

Sweet corn 'Swift'

Lettuce 'Salad Bowl Mixed'

Cabbage 'Marner Early Red'

Pretty potager

Formal patterns and exquisite color combinations characterize the French-style potager, where vegetables look as attractive as ornamental plants.

Planting a potager is not difficult, but it does require careful planning to select and arrange colored varieties that mature to provide interest throughout the year. Here, sweet corn and runner beans add valuable height to a scheme dominated by gray and purple foliage.

Border basics

Size 20 x 25 ft (6 x 8 m)

Suits An area with easy wheelbarrow access and a water supply

Soil Fertile, moist, and free-draining

Site Large open plot in full sun, with shelter from strong winds

Shopping list

- 1 x packet runner bean 'Liberty' seed
- 1 x packet sweet corn 'Lark' seed
- 1 x packet cabbage 'Red Jewel' seed
- 1 x packet fava bean 'The Sutton' seed
- 1 x packet kale 'Red Russian' seed
- 1 x pack shallot 'Golden Gourmet' sets

Planting and aftercare

Prepare the soil by adding plenty of well-rotted manure the fall before planting. Draw out your design on paper, calculating the number of plants required to fill each row and what they can be replaced with once harvested. Plant the seeds in spring, harden off where required, and transplant into neat rows in early summer, adding supports for the runner beans. Water the young plants well, tie climbers to supports, and protect from pests as necessary. Harvest crops as they mature and plan to have replacement plants ready to fill the empty ground as soon as possible to maintain the garden's appearance.

Runner bean 'Liberty'

Sweet corn 'Lark'

Cabbage 'Red Jewel'

Fava bean 'The Sutton'

Kale 'Red Russian'

Shallot 'Golden Gourmet'

Caring for your crops

Taking care of your garden is a year-round task that becomes easier as you learn about your local climate and the requirements of different plants. In this chapter, discover how to weed and water effectively, and how to spot other problems and deal with them appropriately. If, like many vegetable gardeners, you prefer not to use chemicals, there are also tips on luring into your yard a range of beneficial creatures that prey on crop pests.

Garden allies

Some wild creatures help to pollinate plants, break down compost, and prey on pests, so make these friendly visitors welcome in your garden.

Busy bees The flowers of many vegetables, such as runner beans, need to be pollinated by insects in order to set their crop. Bees are excellent pollinators, so include ornamental flowers in your vegetable garden to entice them in.

Friendly pest predators

Not all insects found in the vegetable garden are pests, and many of them prey on harmful insects that can destroy entire crops if left unchecked. It is, therefore, well worthwhile encouraging the good guys into your vegetable garden to try to achieve a natural balance and keep pest numbers low. Remember, too, that many pesticide sprays, even organic ones, kill beneficial insects as well as pests, so are best used only as a last resort.

Hoverflies Sometimes mistaken for bees, adult hoverflies are great pollinators, while the larvae feed voraciously on insect pests.

Ladybugs The adults are familiar friends, but the less appealing larvae enjoy nothing better than feasting on juicy aphids.

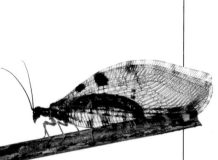

Lacewings The delicate appearance of the adult lacewing belies the enormous appetites of its larvae for common garden pests.

Helpful animals and birds

Although they may be elusive, many larger garden residents, such as birds and toads, can be a gardener's best friend, feeding on slugs and all kinds of other unwelcome visitors. Birds soon flock to gardens where food is provided, and different species will pick off insects and even feed on snails during a visit. Create suitable habitats for all kinds of creatures and they will repay you with a healthier and more productive garden.

Song thrushes These birds break snails from their shells, so plant a berry-bearing shrub or tree on your patch to give them winter food, too.

Brandling worms Smaller and redder than the usual earthworm, these creatures rapidly reduce vegetable matter to compost.

Frogs and toads Even a small pond can become home to a number of frogs and toads, which will help to keep the slug population in check.

Ways to weed

In a vegetable garden, weeds are definitely plants in the wrong place, competing with crops for water, nutrients, and light, as well as harboring pests and diseases that could spread to crops.

Weed control Regular weeding should have all but the wildest sites under control surprisingly quickly and, after a few years, maintenance should be easy. Tackling the work in small sections can help to make it more manageable, too.

Gardeners who prefer not to use chemical herbicides quickly become skilled at weeding with a fork and hoe. The hoe is ideal for clearing larger areas of annual weed seedlings, while a fork is best for uprooting every fragment of pernicious perennial weeds. A hand fork is useful for weeding in between crops.

An organic mulch of straw suppresses weed growth and also looks attractive.

A sheet mulch, such as synthetic landscape fabric, works well for large areas.

Suppressing weed growth Weeds are opportunists that thrive on bare soil, which is difficult to avoid after harvest and when seeds are newly sown. Covering or filling the soil, though, makes it difficult for weeds to grow. Landscape fabric or black plastic over the soil blocks out light, limiting weed growth, and crops can be planted in holes cut through it. A thick organic mulch around young plants also helps to prevent weeds from establishing, while filling gaps between rows with fast-maturing crops like lettuce, or scrambling plants, such as nasturtiums, leaves less space for weeds.

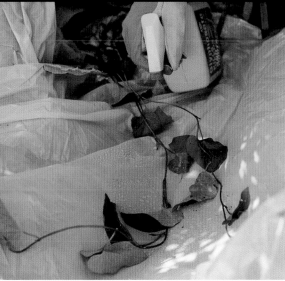

Hoeing Control flushes of annual weeds by pushing a hoe through the top of the soil to sever them from their roots. Shallow hoeing stops more weed seeds being brought to the surface and minimizes moisture loss from the soil. Hoe frequently between rows of germinated seedlings.

Chemical controls Where perennial weeds are a problem, you can use a systemic herbicide that is transferred from the leaves to the roots, killing the whole plant. Apply on a still day and cover up nearby crops with plastic sheeting. Place the weeds on the plastic and spray.

Hand weeding Regular weeding with a hand fork is the best way to keep soil clear around established plants and catch perennial weeds, like this creeping buttercup, while they are still small. Don't leave pulled weeds on the soil, where they may re-root in damp weather or disperse seed.

Tackling perennial weeds These weeds are eradicated only by meticulous digging to remove every last scrap of their spreading roots and runners, or by applying a systemic herbicide. Don't add the weeds to your compost pile or you may spread them back onto your soil.

Gallery of weeds

Perennial weeds

Field bindweed (*Convolvulus arvensis*) This climber, with its pretty white flowers and heart-shaped leaves, will regrow from the tiniest fragment of root and quickly spread.

Bramble (*Rubus*) A scrambling shrub, with long, arching, prickly stems, that can rapidly become invasive and hard to remove. The stems also re-root at the tips.

Creeping buttercup (*Ranunculus repens*) This low-growing plant with yellow flowers spreads by runners that form a dense mat of shallow roots, which are relatively easy to remove.

Couch grass (*Agropyron repens*) This leafy grass spreads incredibly fast by tough, underground roots that can be hard to dig up intact. It will regrow from any pieces left in the soil.

Dandelion (*Taraxacum officinale*) Catch the rosettes of toothed leaves while small and easy to remove— once the taproot grows and the seed disperse, the job is much harder.

Dock (*Rumex*) Large pointed leaves and tall flower spikes grow above a fleshy tap root that extends deep into the soil and takes considerable effort to remove once established.

Ground elder (*Aegopodium podagraria*) The creeping roots make this a pernicious garden weed, easily recognized by its elderlike leaves and clouds of white flowers.

Stinging nettle (*Urtica dioica*) The coarse, jagged leaves are covered with stinging hairs. The bright yellow, creeping roots are easy to see, but a challenge to remove.

Horsetail (*Equisetum*) Almost impossible to eradicate, the dark brown, bootlacelike roots of these feathery plants can extend several yards (meters) underground.

Annual and biennial weeds

Annual meadowgrass (*Poa annua*) This insignificant-looking, low-growing grass colonizes any available space, including cracks in paving, so remove it before it sets seed.

Ragwort (*Senecio jacobaea*) The yellow daisy flowers of this tall plant are produced in its second year, followed by fluffy white seeds that colonize open ground.

Common chickweed (*Stellaria media*) Rather delicate, with charming little white, starlike flowers, this weed establishes and sets seed rapidly, and its sprawling habit smothers seedlings.

Groundsel (*Senecio vulgaris*) The white fluffy seeds of this weed float on the breeze, so it can spread far and wide. Remove plants before the tiny yellow flowers mature.

Shepherd's purse (*Capsella-bursa pastoris*) A rosette of cut-edged leaves gives rise to a spike of small white flowers, which quickly form heart-shaped seed capsules.

Hairy bittercress (*Cardamine hirsuta*) Best pulled up as a seedling, when it has small, watercress-like leaves, because the flower stem rapidly forms long seed pods.

Cleavers (*Galium aparine*) This scrambling weed is covered with little hooked bristles that enable it to climb through plants. Uproot it rather than pulling the stems.

Fat hen (*Chenopodium album*) The gray-green, diamond-shaped leaves of this common weed are easily recognized. It quickly grows tall, with a loose flower spike at its tip.

Plantain (*Plantago*) Low-growing rosettes of almost leathery leaves turn up in beds, paving, and lawns. Remove them before the little bottlebrush flowers are produced.

Dealing with pests

Every garden has its share of pests, so don't panic and reach for the insecticide spray at every sighting. Healthy plants can usually tolerate them, and some are also food for beneficial insects, which you can encourage into your garden.

A healthy balance Help plants stay healthy by providing plenty of water and rich, well-drained soil, and prevent a buildup of pests by planting each crop in a different part of the garden every year. Encourage beneficial creatures, such as birds, hoverflies, and frogs, with suitable food and habitats. This helps achieve a natural balance, where predators keep pest numbers at an acceptable level, and there is less need for chemical intervention.

Control strategies Check plants regularly and pick off any unwelcome arrivals immediately. If you anticipate a problem, put a barrier, such as horticultural fleece for carrot flies, in place, or grow companion plants alongside the crop to entice beneficial insects or confuse pests. If necessary, use chemical sprays in the evening when bees and other beneficial insects are not flying. Sticky sheets are useful in the greenhouse, as are biological controls, which introduce a predatory organism to kill the pests.

Sticky sheets in the greenhouse help to control airborne pests.

Keeping out animal pests

Large animal pests can devastate a vegetable patch overnight, so where you anticipate a problem, the best way to stop them from reaching your plants is to create a physical barrier. Deer and rabbits need fences to keep them at bay, but there are a number of cheap and easy ways of outwitting slugs, snails, mice, and birds.

- Halved plastic bottles with copper tape around the base protect young plants from slugs, snails, and birds.
- Netting supported with canes or wire keeps out birds; a fine net separates egg-laying butterflies from brassicas.
- Tightly secured netting deters burrowers like rabbits (*see opposite*), which eat roots, brassicas, and peas.

Plastic bottles and copper tape deter slugs.   Prevent bird damage with netting.   Horticultural fleece keeps out carrot flies.

Gallery of pests

Aphids Sap-sucking insects (greenflies, blackflies) weaken growth and carry diseases. Encourage birds and insect predators, pick off small groups, or use a suitable insecticide.

Rabbits Keep these voracious vegetable eaters out of the garden with a small-meshed fence that extends 1 ft (30 cm) underground to prevent them from burrowing in.

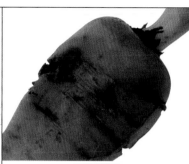

Carrot flies Cover crops with horticultural fleece, sow carefully to reduce the need for thinning, or grow resistant varieties to prevent carrot fly larvae from tunneling into roots.

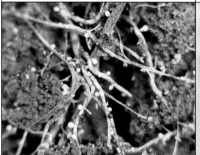

Potato cyst eelworm These microscopic, sap-sucking nematodes cause potato leaves to discolor and die. Avoid replanting the same crop where an infestation has occurred.

Caterpillars Different parts of various plants may be damaged by caterpillars. Pea moth caterpillars (*above*) live inside the pods. Net crops to exclude egg-laying adults.

Flea beetles These tiny black beetles eat round holes in the leaves of brassicas, turnip, radish, and arugula. Keep them at bay by covering seedlings with horticultural fleece.

Whiteflies Treat glasshouse whitefly with the biological control *Encarsia formosa* (parasitic wasp), and the brassica whitefly with a suitable insecticide.

Red spider mites Small mites cause mottling on leaves, particularly in the greenhouse. Mist plants to increase humidity, and use a predatory mite *Phytoseiulus persimilis*.

Slugs and snails Protect vulnerable plants, and try beer traps and flashlight hunts. Nematode biological controls are less harmful to other animals than slug pellets.

Dealing with diseases

Just like people, strong, healthy plants are more able to fight off infection than weak, malnourished ones. Here's how to keep yours in shape.

Prevention is better than cure Good cultivation is as much a part of fighting diseases as recognizing and treating them, and with few fungicides now available to the amateur, preventative measures are essential.

Plants require a ready supply of nutrients and water to sustain healthy growth, so add plenty of organic matter to the soil to release nutrients and help retain moisture. Additional watering may also be needed, particularly in hot weather. It is important not to forget plants under cover and in containers, which rely on regular watering and feeding to sustain them. Damp conditions and poor air circulation can encourage fungal problems, such as damping-off of seedlings, so use free-draining potting mix and provide good ventilation when sowing indoors.

A neat garden also helps to keep diseases at bay. Ensure that sources of infection, such as dead leaves, harvested plants, and nearby weeds, are removed at the first opportunity. Burn or discard any diseased material; don't compost it because infection could spread.

Although not easy in a small garden, it is advisable to practice crop rotation, where related groups of crops are grown together and moved to a new bed each year, helping to prevent the buildup of diseases in the soil (*see p.39*). Where diseases are known to be a problem, try growing resistant varieties. Be aware that plants brought into your garden can introduce disease, so check any purchases or gifts carefully before planting.

Deficiency, not disease Signs of nutrient deficiency, such as yellowing leaves and blossom end rot on tomatoes and peppers, are often mistaken for diseases. Learn to recognize these disorders, so that you can act quickly and minimize their effects. Sometimes the remedy is as simple as improving the water supply; other problems may need fertilizer added to the soil.

Use fresh seed starting mix and new or sterilized pots and trays to prevent damping-off disease.

Keep the garden well watered to encourage vigorous, healthy growth that is less susceptible to all kinds of infection.

Add lime to acidic soils before planting brassicas to increase the pH level and reduce the incidence of clubroot.

Gallery of diseases and disorders

Potato/tomato blight Brown patches on leaves, fruits, and tubers, caused by a fungus that thrives in warm, wet weather. Grow resistant varieties or spray with copper-based fungicide.

Sclerotinia Fungus that causes brown, slimy rot with fluffy, white growth, predominantly on stems and fruits of various vegetables. Remove and burn or discard affected plants.

Magnesium deficiency Older leaves of various vegetables show yellowing between veins, especially in acidic soil or after heavy rains. Apply Epsom salts to the soil or as a foliar spray.

Clubroot This soil-borne slime mold infects brassicas, causing swollen roots, wilting foliage, even death. Ensure good drainage, add lime to acidic soil, and choose resistant varieties.

Blossom end rot Dry conditions affect calcium uptake, which causes sunken, black patches at the tips of tomatoes and sweet peppers. Correct with adequate, regular watering.

Powdery mildew A wide range of crops are affected by these fungi, causing powdery white growth on leaves in dry soil conditions. Water the soil well, but not over the leaves.

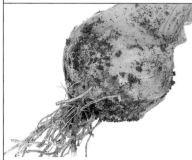

Onion white rot This fungus persists in the soil for up to seven years and causes fluffy white growth on bulbs and roots and yellowing of leaves. Remove and burn infected plants.

Rust Orange or brown spots appear on the leaves and stems of various vegetable crops, particularly in damp weather. Remove infected leaves and grow resistant varieties.

Botrytis A fluffy, gray mold (or whitish spots on tomatoes) that enters plants through wounds or flowers. Remove dead and infected plant material to reduce risk of infection.

Beneficial planting

Gardeners have developed many ways in which to use plants to help outwit pests, attract pollinating insects, and enrich the soil in the vegetable garden.

Companion planting One of the best-known plants to combine with vegetable crops is the French marigold (*Tagetes*). The strong scent of its vividly colored flowers is thought to mask the smell of surrounding crops so that pests cannot detect them. Many gardeners find it effective outdoors and also in the greenhouse.

Enrich the soil and attract insects Plants known as green manures (*below left*) are grown for digging back into the soil to add valuable nitrogen and organic material. In small gardens they are best used in conjunction with compost and other organic matter, and dug in before they set seed and become woody. Plants that flower prolifically, such as *Limnanthes* (*below right*), are ideal for attracting beneficial insects and add welcome splashes of color, too.

Green manures, such as winter tare, are dug back into the soil.

Beneficial insects flock to the bright flowers of *Limnanthes douglasii*.

Intercropping Working in the same way as companion planting, the strong scent of this crop of onions is thought to overpower the scent of carrots, causing carrot flies to bypass the crop and leave it undamaged.

Grow sacrificial basil Help limit whitefly damage to greenhouse crops by planting basil alongside them. The whitefly usually attacks the tender basil leaves first, leaving crop plants relatively unscathed.

Seasonal planner

Gardening is governed by the seasons, and timing tasks correctly for your climate and soil will increase the chance of bumper crops throughout the year.

Spring

As the weather warms and the days lengthen, vegetable gardeners are always eager to get growing. However, it is a good idea to find out the average date of the last frost in your area and not to sow any tender crops under cover until 4–6 weeks before this date. This gives plants time to grow to a good size for transplanting and hardening off, without their getting too large or leggy.

Sowing and planting outdoors Many hardy vegetables can be sown directly into sun-warmed prepared soil.
- Early spring: sow fava beans, Brussels sprouts, cabbages, green onions, kale, leeks, lettuce, onions, parsley, parsnips, peas, summer cauliflowers; plant asparagus, globe and Jerusalem artichokes, early potatoes, garlic, onion and shallot sets.
- Mid-spring: sow arugula, beets, purple sprouting broccoli, cabbages, calabrese, carrots, cauliflowers, kohlrabi, leeks, lettuce, peas, radishes, spinach, Swiss chard, turnips; plant globe and Jerusalem artichokes, onion sets, potatoes.
- Late spring: sow arugula, cabbages, cauliflowers, carrots, French and runner beans, lettuces, parsnips, peas, radishes, sweet corn, Swiss chard.

Sowing under cover Sow hardy vegetables under glass for an early crop, and give tender vegetables a head start with protection from unpredictable spring weather.

- Early spring: arugula, basil, beets, carrots, celeriac, celery, cucumbers, eggplants, lettuce, parsley, peppers, tomatoes.
- Mid-spring: basil, celeriac, celery, cucumbers, eggplants, French and runner beans, parsley, peppers, sweet corn, tomatoes.
- Late spring: squash, summer squash, zucchini.

Harvesting Harvest overwintered brassicas, and pick crops that have been grown under cover (see pp.34–35).
- Early spring: cabbages, cauliflower, evergreen herbs, kale, purple sprouting broccoli, salad leaves.
- Mid-spring: cauliflower, evergreen herbs, kale, purple sprouting broccoli, salad leaves, Swiss chard.
- Late spring: asparagus, fava beans, green onions, kohlrabi, peas, perennial herbs, radishes, salad leaves.

Seasonal jobs There are plenty of tasks to keep you busy at this time of year, so make the most of good weather.
- Prick out and pot on seedlings as soon as they are large enough to handle. Harden off young plants as the risk of frost decreases.
- Hoe to control weeds; prepare beds for planting; put up supports for peas and beans; lift and divide perennial herbs; repot herbs in containers; water plants in pots.
- Earth up potatoes to protect from frost and cover early crops with cloches or fleece to keep out the cold; protect young brassicas from birds.

Spring is the time to start sowing seeds in drills outdoors. | French and runner beans can be sown outdoors in late spring.

Seasonal planner *continued*

Summer

Try to make a little time every day for weeding, watering, and harvesting. Even in tiny gardens, gluts of vegetables are possible, so sow small amounts of seeds successionally every 2–3 weeks to ensure a steady supply over summer.

Sowing Keep up successional sowings throughout the summer, and don't forget those late summer sowings that can be protected with cloches and harvested in winter.
- Early summer: arugula, beets, calabrese, carrots, outdoor cucumbers, French and runner beans, green onions, herbs, lettuce, peas, radishes, rutabagas, squash, Swiss chard, turnips, zucchini.
- Midsummer: Asian greens, beets, calabrese, lettuce, green onions, turnips.
- Late summer: Asian greens, radishes, spinach, spring cabbages, turnips, winter radishes.

Transplanting In early summer, transplant into their final positions young plants raised under cover or outdoors in seedbeds. Ensure tender crops are not placed outside until the risk of frost has passed. Some tender types are best grown indoors. Make sure that you water transplants well.
- Indoors: cucumbers, eggplants, peppers, tomatoes.
- Outdoors: Brussels sprouts, cabbages, cauliflowers, celeriac, celery, French and runner beans, kale, leeks, purple sprouting broccoli, sweet corn, tomatoes, winter squash, zucchini.

Harvesting Frequent picking encourages many plants to produce more flowers and crop for longer.
- Early summer: beets, cabbages, cauliflower, fava beans, globe artichokes, green onions, herbs, kohlrabi, lettuce, peas, early potatoes, radishes, salad leaves, Swiss chard, turnips, zucchini.
- Midsummer: beets, cabbages, carrots, cucumbers, fava beans, garlic, green onions, herbs, kohlrabi, lettuce, peas, early potatoes, radishes, salad leaves, and tomatoes, zucchini.
- Late summer: cabbages, carrots, calabrese, chili peppers, cucumbers, French and runner beans, eggplants, herbs, lettuce, onions, peas, peppers, salad leaves, second early potatoes, shallots, sweet corn, tomatoes, zucchini.

Seasonal jobs Raising strong plants and caring for them well helps to maintain a healthy and productive garden.
- Keep the garden neat, and water, fertilize, and weed all plants regularly. If you go on vacation, enlist the help of a friend or neighbor while you are away.
- In early summer apply a thin mix of shading whitewash to greenhouse glass. Monitor greenhouse ventilation daily and keep watch for signs of pests and diseases.
- Train climbing vegetables onto their supports, remove sideshoots from cordon tomatoes, and earth up maincrop potatoes and tall brassicas.
- Be ready to store any vegetables and herbs that you cannot use fresh.

Provide shade for greenhouse crops with a thin mix of whitewash.

Earth up maincrop potatoes to exclude light from the tubers.

Fall

The vegetable garden is still full of life, with plenty left to harvest and lots of seeds to sow for early crops next year.

Sowing, planting, and transplanting
- Early fall: sow under cover Asian salad leaves, Japanese onions, spinach, Swiss chard; transplant spring cabbages.
- Mid-fall: sow calabrese, carrots, fava beans, peas.
- Late fall: sow fava beans, hardy lettuce; plant garlic cloves.

Harvesting
- Early fall: beets, carrots, chili peppers, cucumbers, French and runner beans, peppers, maincrop potatoes, salad leaves, sweet corn, tomatoes, winter squash.
- Mid-fall: cabbages, carrots, maincrop potatoes, salad leaves, tomatoes, turnips.
- Late fall: cabbages, herbs, kale, leeks, parsnips, salad leaves.

Seasonal jobs
- Tidy up the garden, removing all annual, non-seeding weeds and spent crop plants to the compost pile.
- Cure squashes so they store well.
- Wash shading paint from greenhouse glass.
- Remove lower leaves of tomato plants to help the last fruits ripen.

Winter

Although this is the season to catch your breath, remember to consider the year's successes and failures and use your experience to help choose suitable crops for next season.

Sowing and planting Hardy crops can be sown as early as midwinter under cover.
- Midwinter: sow early cauliflowers, early carrots, fava beans, leeks, lettuce, onions, shallots.
- Late winter: sow Brussels sprouts, summer cabbages, fava beans, leeks, onions, peas, radishes, shallots, turnips; plant Jerusalem artichokes.

Harvesting
- Brussels sprouts, cabbages, kale, leeks, parsnips; under cover: salad leaves, especially Asian greens and chard.

Seasonal jobs If you want to change the garden layout, this is the time to build paths, raised beds, or other features, so they are ready for spring planting.
- Order seeds, seed potatoes, and onion sets. Begin chitting first early seed potatoes in midwinter in a cool, light place.
- Dig and manure the soil in fine weather as it becomes free of crops; apply lime where necessary.
- Wash down the greenhouse and staging with horticultural detergent, and clear away old plant material to prevent the spread of pests and diseases.

Braid garlic leaves together to display your harvest.

Winter is the time to dig your soil and control weeds.

Plant guide

Open any seed catalog and you will
see a huge range of vegetables.
With dozens of varieties to choose
from, the right selection can mean
the difference between success and
disappointment, so use this guide to
determine what will suit you best.
The symbols below are used
throughout the guide to indicate the
conditions each crop requires.

Key to plant symbols

Soil preference

◊ Well-drained soil

◔ Moist soil

◆ Wet soil

Preference for sun or shade

☼ Full sun

☼ Partial or dappled shade

☀ Full shade

Root vegetables: potatoes

Potato 'Red Duke of York'
A vigorous first early, producing abundant, good-sized, red-skinned tubers with delicious pale yellow flesh. Perfect in salads when small, and boiled or baked when larger. Young shoots need protection from frost.

Plant: early spring
Harvest: early to midsummer
◊ ◊ ☼

Potato 'Foremost'
Harvest this useful early variety from early summer or lift as required throughout the summer. The white-skinned, white-fleshed crop has a firm texture, ideal for salads and boiling. Protect young shoots from frost.

Plant: early spring
Harvest: early to late summer
◊ ◊ ☼

Potato 'Arran Pilot'
A popular first early, excellent for gardeners eager to enjoy large yields of small potatoes with creamy, waxy flesh. Good scab resistance and tolerance of dry spells. Young shoots need protection from frost.

Plant: early spring
Harvest: early to midsummer
◊ ◊ ☼

Potato 'Mimi'
The ideal first early for containers, producing masses of small red tubers with incredibly tasty, waxy, cream-colored flesh. An excellent salad potato with good scab resistance. Protect new shoots from frost.

Plant: early spring
Harvest: early summer
◊ ◊ ☼

Potato 'Charlotte'
A supermarket favorite because of its long, smooth, yellow tubers, with fabulously flavored, waxy flesh. This second early is easy to grow in the garden, and one of the best salad potatoes.

Plant: mid-spring
Harvest: mid- to late summer
◊ ◊ ☼

Potato 'Saxon'
For baking, boiling, and french-frying, try this floury textured second early. The large, white tubers have a mild, creamy flavor, and the plants display a useful resistance to both blackleg and eelworm.

Plant: mid-spring
Harvest: mid- to late summer
◊ ◊ ☼

Potato 'Royal Kidney'
An old maincrop salad variety, 'Royal Kidney' produces delicious, yellow-fleshed salad potatoes from late summer. It is also tempting to dig up the plants earlier for crops of tender baby potatoes.

Plant: mid-spring
Harvest: late summer
◊ ◗ ☼

Potato 'Ratte'
The long, slightly knobby tubers harvested from this maincrop variety are a real treat. Their dense, waxy, yellow flesh has a strong nutty flavor, making them perfect for salads.

Plant: mid-spring
Harvest: late summer
◊ ◗ ☼

Potato 'Pink Fir Apple'
A curious old maincrop variety, producing long, irregular tubers with pink-tinged skin that is best left on during cooking. The waxy flesh, with its earthy flavor, is popular in salads, and the tubers store well.

Plant: mid-spring
Harvest: from early fall
◊ ◗ ☼

Potato 'Kerrs Pink'
This versatile and high-yielding maincrop variety is reliable in most soils. The blush pink tubers have delicious floury cream flesh that is perfect for mashing, french-frying, roasting, and baking. Stores well.

Plant: mid-spring
Harvest: from early fall
◊ ◗ ☼

Potato 'Sante'
An excellent choice for organic gardeners because of its excellent pest and disease resistance, this maincrop variety yields large cream tubers that are great for baking, boiling, and roasting. Stores well.

Plant: mid-spring
Harvest: from late summer
◊ ◗ ☼

Potato 'Nicola'
Resistance to eelworm and blight makes this variety a good option for maincrop salad potatoes. Large crops of long, yellow, waxy tubers are reliably produced and store well over winter.

Plant: mid-spring
Harvest: from late summer
◊ ◗ ☼

Root vegetables: carrots, beets, parsnips

Carrot *'Parmex'*
Dumpy, spherical roots make this one of the best carrots for sowing into patio pots or shallow soil. Despite their shape, they have a fine sweet flavor. The earliest crops can be sown under glass or protected with cloches.

Sow: early to late spring
Harvest: late spring to early fall
◊ ☼

Carrot *'Infinity'* F1
This late maincrop carrot has an elegant, slender root that is delicious raw or cooked. The sweet carrots are deep orange right to their core and keep well in the soil into fall or can be lifted and stored successfully.

Sow: early spring to midsummer
Harvest: late summer to late fall
◊ ☼

Carrot *'Flyaway'* F1
Specially bred to be less prone to attack by carrot flies, this maincrop carrot produces good crops where the pest would render others inedible. The stout, cylindrical roots are smooth-skinned and sugary.

Sow: early spring to midsummer
Harvest: late spring to mid-fall
◊ ☼

Carrot *'Purple Haze'* F1
As its name suggests, this variety has unconventional dark purple roots, which reveal contrasting orange cores when they are sliced. Flavor is not sacrificed and is particularly good when raw.

Sow: early spring to early summer
Harvest: early summer to late fall
◊ ☼

Carrot *'Bangor'* F1
Long, stocky roots are produced in large quantities, especially in moist soil, by this excellent maincrop variety. Crops can be harvested from late summer and throughout fall, and store well once lifted.

Sow: mid-spring to early summer
Harvest: midsummer to late fall
◊ ☼

Carrot *'Carson'* F1
Fall and winter bring good crops of this medium-sized, tapering variety. The rich orange color, combined with the delicious crunchy texture and sweetness, makes them irresistible when eaten raw.

Sow: mid-spring to midsummer
Harvest: late summer to early winter
◊ ☼

Beet 'Boltardy'

A reliable variety yielding traditional deep red globe-shaped roots with a fine sweet flavor. Perfect for sowing under cloches in early spring because of its excellent resistance to bolting.

Sow: early spring to midsummer
Harvest: early summer to mid-fall
○ ☼

Beet 'Chioggia Pink'

A beautiful curiosity; the rich red skin of this spherical root conceals flesh marked with concentric rings of blush pink and white. Its sweet, mild flavor is delightful raw or cooked.

Sow: mid-spring to midsummer.
Harvest: early summer to mid-fall
○ ☼

Beet 'Forono'

Elongated, burgundy-colored roots make this variety ideal for slicing. Tender young roots have a particularly intense flavor, so sow successionally for a continuous supply. Prone to bolting if sown too early.

Sow: mid-spring to early summer
Harvest: midsummer to late fall
○ ☼

Beet 'Pablo' F1

One of the best varieties for growing in patio containers and perfect to harvest as baby beets. The smooth, deep red, spherical roots taste exceptionally sweet; they also stand well in the soil without bolting or becoming woody.

Sow: mid-spring to early summer
Harvest: midsummer to mid-fall
○ ☼

Parsnip 'Gladiator' F1

A popular hybrid parsnip that matures quickly, producing consistently reliable, early-maturing crops of white-skinned roots. 'Gladiator' also benefits from good canker resistance.

Sow: late winter to mid-spring
Harvest: mid-fall to early spring
○ ☼

Parsnip 'Tender and True'

In deep soil, this variety forms exceptionally long roots, which are often considered to have one of the finest parsnip flavors. It is also resistant to canker and is a firm favorite with exhibition growers.

Sow: late winter to mid-spring
Harvest: late fall to early spring
○ ☼

Root vegetables: turnips, rutabagas, radishes

Turnip '*Snowball*'
For a quick crop, this fast-maturing variety is one of the best. The pure white globes are best harvested while young, when their deliciously crisp, firm, white flesh can be enjoyed raw or cooked.

Sow: early spring to midsummer
Harvest: late spring onward
◌ ◗ ☼ ☀

Turnip '*Purple Top Milan*'
A good choice for early sowings under cloches, this turnip crops reliably and matures quickly. The flat-topped roots are a vivid shade of purple above the soil and pure white beneath it, making them attractive as well as delicious.

Sow: early spring to midsummer
Harvest: mid-spring onward
◌ ◗ ☼ ☀

Rutabaga '*Brora*'
This gem among rutabagas has the classic purple top and cream base, but has been bred to produce the finest smooth flesh without any bitterness. Best harvested in early winter to avoid woodiness.

Sow: late spring to midsummer
Harvest: mid-fall to midwinter
◌ ☼

Radish '*French Breakfast*'
A torpedo-shaped variety with rosy red skin and a bright white tip. Its shape makes it great for slicing, and the crunchy flesh has a mild flavor with just a hint of peppery heat. Easy and quick to grow.

Sow: early spring to early summer
Harvest: late spring to mid-fall
◌ ◗ ☼ ☀

Radish '*Cherry Belle*'
Probably one of the best vegetables for the absolute beginner, these small, round, brilliant red radishes tolerate poor-quality soil. They grow rapidly, are slow to become woody, and have tasty, mild-flavored flesh.

Sow: early spring to early summer
Harvest: late spring to mid-fall
◌ ◗ ☼ ☀

Chinese radish '*Mantanghong*' **F1**
For a taste of the exotic, try these easy-to-grow, tennis-ball-sized radishes. Their plain, pale green skin hides vivid magenta flesh with a white outer layer, which has a nutty flavor and a touch of heat.

Sow: early summer to midsummer
Harvest: late summer to early winter
◌ ◗ ☼ ☀

Brassicas: cabbages

Cabbage 'Pixie'
One of the earliest pointed cabbages, which can be picked young as spring greens or allowed to mature into a firm-hearted cabbage. A reliable crop that can be harvested in time to leave soil clear for spring sowings.

Sow: midsummer
Harvest: midwinter to late spring
◊ ◖ ☼ ☀

Cabbage 'Derby Day'
A traditional, pale green ballhead cabbage for early summer harvest. Its resistance to bolting has long made it popular with gardeners, and the mature cabbages can stand even summer heat.

Sow: late winter to early spring
Harvest: early to late summer
◊ ◖ ☼ ☀

Cabbage 'Hispi' F1
Another favorite, this pointed cabbage reliably produces compact, tasty, dark green heads. The cabbages mature rapidly, and successional sowings provide a harvest from late spring into fall.

Sow: late winter to late summer
Harvest: late spring to late fall
◊ ◖ ☼ ☀

Cabbage 'Marner Early Red' (syn. 'Marner Fruerot')
This dense-hearted cabbage is one of the first reds to reach maturity. The outer leaves are tinged with gray; the head is an intense red and has a peppery flavor best appreciated raw.

Sow: midwinter to early spring
Harvest: midsummer to late summer
◊ ◖ ☼ ☀

Cabbage 'Minicole' F1
Ideal for small gardens, this white ballhead cabbage produces small, uniform heads on compact plants. Plant closely for a bumper harvest of fall cabbages, which will stand in the ground for up to three months.

Sow: early to late spring
Harvest: early fall to early winter
◊ ◖ ☼ ☀

Cabbage 'Red Jewel' F1
The claret-colored leaves dusted with silver make this one of the best cabbages for ornamental plantings. The tight round heads also taste delicious and will stand in the ground well or store indoors.

Sow: early spring to early summer
Harvest: midsummer to early fall
◊ ◖ ☼ ☀

Brassicas: cabbages, calabrese, broccoli, cauliflower

Cabbage *'January King 3'*

This traditional winter cabbage has good frost resistance and appetizing sweet crunchy leaves. The frilly-edged leaves are tinged with pink and also look beautiful in the winter garden.

Sow: mid-spring to early summer
Harvest: late fall to late winter
◊ ◊ ☼ ☀

Cabbage *'Tundra'* **F1**

A cross between a savoy and a white cabbage, this extremely hardy variety produces solid round heads of tasty crisp leaves. The long cropping season makes this a really useful addition to the vegetable patch.

Sow: early spring to early summer
Harvest: mid-fall to early spring
◊ ◊ ☼ ☀

Cabbage *'Savoy Siberia'* **F1**

A truly tough vegetable, this savoy withstands hard winters, so is ideal for exposed or cold gardens. The blue-green, blistered leaves taste sweet, and the cabbages stand well in the ground for long periods.

Sow: early spring to early summer
Harvest: early fall to midwinter
◊ ◊ ☼ ☀

Calabrese *'Corvet'* **F1**

A reliable variety of fall vegetable, producing robust plants and a bumper crop of dense, green heads. Cut the central head while its flowers are still tightly closed for a second harvest of smaller shoots a few weeks later.

Sow: mid- to late spring
Harvest: late summer to early fall
◊ ◊ ☼

Broccoli *'Bordeaux'*

This purple sprouting variety is very useful for those who can't wait until spring for broccoli. It is not winter-hardy and does not require the usual exposure to cold to produce its tasty spears.

Sow: late winter to mid-spring
Harvest: midsummer to mid-fall
◊ ☼

Broccoli *'White Star'*

Creamy white rather than purple flowers make the spears of this spring variety reminiscent of cauliflower; many consider the taste similar, too. Reliably high yields produced over a long period make it a popular choice.

Sow: mid- to late spring
Harvest: early to mid-spring
◊ ☼

Broccoli *'Claret'* **F1**

A large, vigorous plant that may need staking in windy gardens, this variety produces huge yields of chunky, succulent spears in spring. The purple flowerheads are tightly packed and uniform, and taste delicious.

Sow: mid- to late spring
Harvest: early to mid-spring
◊ ☼

Broccoli *'Late Purple Sprouting'*

To extend your broccoli crop into late spring, try this slightly later-flowering variety. It is slow to go to seed, and the delicious purple-budded spears can be cut over a long period.

Sow: mid- to late spring
Harvest: early to late spring
◊ ☼

Cauliflower *'Walcheran Winter Armado April'*

An extremely hardy winter variety that tolerates heavy frosts and produces large, solid, pure white heads. It ties up a bed for 12 months, so may not be suitable for very small gardens.

Sow: mid- to late spring
Harvest: early to late spring
◊ ◑ ☼

Cauliflower *'Mayflower'* **F1**

High-quality, dense white curds are consistently produced by this vigorous early summer variety. Unlike many others, it does not require high nitrogen levels and is harvested early enough to avoid midsummer droughts.

Sow: mid- to late winter and mid-fall **Harvest:** late spring to midsummer ◊ ◑ ☼

Cauliflower *'Romanesco'*

If you want something different, try this strange summer/fall variety, with pyramid-shaped heads in a vibrant shade of acid green. Grow over a long season for large heads or sow successionally for frequent small crops.

Sow: early to late spring
Harvest: late summer to early winter
◊ ◑ ☼

Cauliflower *'Violet Queen'* **F1**

The vivid purple curds formed by this variety will brighten up any vegetable patch, although they turn green when cooked. Plenty of nitrogen and water are required to sustain strong growth.

Sow: late spring to early summer
Harvest: late summer to early fall
◊ ◑ ☼

Brassicas: Brussels sprouts, kale, kohlrabi, Asian greens

Brussels sprouts *'Red Delicious'*

This magnificent variety is a striking shade of red-tinged-purple from its crowning leaves to the base of its stem. Unlike many other red varieties, the sprouts retain their color after cooking and have a fine flavor.

Sow: early to mid-spring
Harvest: early winter
◌ ◌ ☼

Brussels sprouts *'Trafalgar'* **F1**

If your aim is sweet sprouts for Christmas, then this variety will not disappoint. Dense crops of firm, uniformly-sized sprouts grow on tall, sturdy plants and can be harvested throughout the winter.

Sow: early to mid-spring
Harvest: late fall to midwinter
◌ ◌ ☼

Brussels sprouts *'Bosworth'* **F1**

Dark green, dense, sweet sprouts are produced in abundance by this tough hybrid variety, which will stand well through cold winter weather. Some tolerance to downy mildew helps ensure a healthy crop.

Sow: early to mid-spring
Harvest: late fall to early winter
◌ ◌ ☼

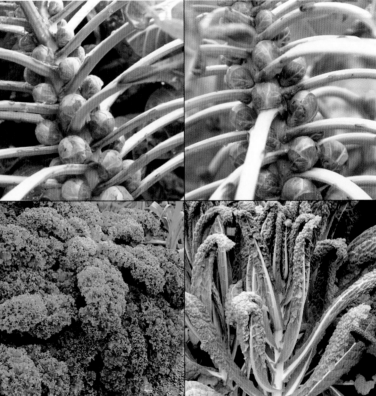

Kale *'Redbor'* **F1**

All kales are useful hardy winter crops, but the tall leaves of this variety resemble large clumps of burgundy, curly-leaved parsley and add some welcome color to dull days. Great steamed or stir-fried.

Sow: early to late spring
Harvest: early fall to early spring
◌ ◌ ☼ ☼

Kale *'Starbor'* **F1**

More compact than most kales, this variety is well suited to the small or windswept garden. The tightly curled green leaves stand up well to winter cold. Try successional sowings for a year-round crop of tasty baby leaves.

Sow: early spring to early summer
Harvest: early fall to early spring
◌ ◌ ☼ ☼

Kale *'Nero di Toscana'*

Also known as Black Tuscany or Cavolo Nero, this is the favored kale in Italian kitchens. Its upright leaves are almost black and blistered like those of savoy cabbages. Use mature leaves in soups and stews, baby ones in salads.

Sow: early spring to early summer
Harvest: early fall to early spring
◌ ◌ ☼ ☼

Kohlrabi 'Olivia' F1

Harvest the swollen stem that sits just above soil level when it is about the size of a tennis ball, and enjoy the crisp, white flesh grated raw in salads or lightly steamed. Reliable, with little woodiness, this variety is slow to bolt.

Sow: early spring to early summer
Harvest: late spring to mid-fall
◌ ◍ ☼ ☀

Kohlrabi 'Purple Danube' F1

The vibrant purple skin and stems of this variety are striking in the garden, and its sweet nutty flavor is one of the best. Purple varieties take longer to mature than white, so this makes a good late summer and fall crop.

Sow: mid-spring to early summer
Harvest: midsummer to late fall
◌ ◍ ☼ ☀

Bok choy 'Joi Choi'

Summer stir-fries will be fresher and tastier with the addition of these succulent, crispy, home-grown leaves. This variety has attractive bright white stems that carry deep green, rounded leaves, and it is easy to grow.

Sow: mid-spring to early fall
Harvest: early summer to mid-fall
◌ ◍ ☼ ☀

Mizuna

Often found in supermarket salad mixes, these jagged-edged, slightly mustard-flavored leaves are simple to cultivate over summer. Harvest baby leaves for salads or allow plants to mature and use leaves for stir-frying.

Sow: early spring to early fall
Harvest: late spring to late fall
◌ ☼

Mibuna

Similar in flavor to mizuna, but with a stronger peppery tang and long, smooth-edged foliage. Like mizuna, this is an ideal cut-and-come-again crop that can be sown successionally from spring to fall.

Sow: early spring to early fall
Harvest: late spring to late fall
◌ ☼

Mustard 'Red Giant'

Another beautiful, strongly flavored leaf, this ruby-tinged mustard is best harvested while the leaves are small, otherwise the peppery flavor can be overpowering. Hardy enough to stand over winter from an fall sowing.

Sow: early spring to early fall
Harvest: late spring to midwinter
◌ ☼

Salad and leafy vegetables: lettuce, spinach, arugula

Lettuce *'Sangria'*

This butterhead type matures to form a loose heart with soft leaves, and a pretty red flush that will brighten up a salad. Easy to grow and quick to mature, it does well in poorer soil and has some resistance to mildew.

Sow: early spring to late summer
Harvest: late spring to mid-fall
◊ ◊ ☼ ☀

Lettuce *'Tom Thumb'*

A gardeners' favorite, this compact, green, butterhead lettuce rapidly forms dense, sweet-tasting hearts. Ideal for small gardens because it can be planted at high densities and is ready for harvest quickly.

Sow: early spring to midsummer
Harvest: late spring to early fall
◊ ◊ ☼ ☀

Lettuce *'Little Gem'*

This cos lettuce is familiar from the supermarket shelves, but is even crisper and sweeter if you grow it yourself. Its diminutive size makes it perfect for small gardens, and it is one of the fastest-cropping cos types.

Sow: early spring to midsummer
Harvest: late spring to early fall
◊ ◊ ☼ ☀

Lettuce *'Freckles'*

This semi-cos variety forms an open head with green leaves that are spectacularly splattered with red. A good choice for flower borders, where it matures quickly. Plants are slow to bolt, even in warm weather.

Sow: early spring to late summer
Harvest: late spring to mid-fall
◊ ◊ ☼ ☀

Lettuce *'Delicato'*

Loose leaf lettuces are the quickest and easiest to grow, either as cut-and-come-again baby leaves or for harvesting whole when mature. This deep red oakleaf variety has a pleasant flavor.

Sow: early spring to midsummer
Harvest: mid-spring to mid-fall
◊ ◊ ☼ ☀

Lettuce *'Catalogna'*

A tasty, green, oakleaf lettuce that you will not want to forget to sow successionally all through summer. The tender leaves have a fine flavor and the non-hearting plants are slow to bolt, should they get the chance.

Sow: early spring to midsummer
Harvest: mid-spring to mid-fall
◊ ◊ ☼ ☀

Lettuce 'Lollo Rossa-Nika'
The red leaves of this frilled lettuce are so dark as to be almost purple and are incredibly ornamental as well as appetizing. Young leaves taste sweet, and, although they turn bitter as they grow, the curled heads look fabulous.

Sow: early spring to midsummer
Harvest: late spring to mid-fall
◌ ◌ ☼ ☀

Lettuce 'Challenge'
Crisphead lettuces are similar to the iceberg types. This reliable variety forms large, solid hearts of crunchy leaves and performs well when sown early and late under cloches. Good resistance to mildew and bolting.

Sow: early spring to midsummer
Harvest: late spring to mid-fall
◌ ◌ ☼ ☀

Lettuce 'Sioux'
A pretty red-tinged iceberg variety, with leaves that intensify in color in warmer weather, giving the plants good ornamental qualities that are so valuable in small gardens. Perfect color and crunch for salads.

Sow: early spring to midsummer
Harvest: early summer to mid-fall
◌ ◌ ☼ ☀

Spinach 'Perpetual Spinach'
Not a true spinach, but spinach beet, with a taste similar to Swiss chard. It is easy to grow because it rarely runs to seed, even in dry conditions. Succulent green leaves are produced prolifically and crops can be gathered all winter.

Sow: mid-spring to midsummer
Harvest: any time
◌ ◌ ☼

Spinach 'Tetona' F1
A high-yielding spinach producing a profusion of rounded dark green leaves. This is the perfect variety for sowing as a cut-and-come-again crop to produce baby leaves for salads, but it can also be left to mature.

Sow: early spring to late summer
Harvest: late spring to late fall
◌ ◌ ☼ ☀

Arugula 'Apollo'
This cultivated variety has large, rounded, green leaves and a strong peppery flavor without any bitterness. The plant is easy to grow as a cut-and-come-again crop in pots or in the ground. Water well in hot weather.

Sow: early spring to midsummer
Harvest: mid-spring to mid-fall
◌ ◌ ☼ ☀

Leafy vegetables: arugula, chicory, Swiss chard

Arugula 'Rocket Wild'
A popular salad leaf with slim, divided leaves and a pungent peppery taste. Easy to grow in pots or beds, it does not bolt as quickly as cultivated forms, but pick the leaves frequently for a longer cropping period.

Sow: early spring to early fall
Harvest: from mid-spring (through winter under cover) ◐ ◌ ☼ ☀

Chicory 'Italiko Rosso'
Red-stemmed asparagus, or catalogna chicory, grows well in poor soil and is ideal for harvesting as baby leaves to add a slightly bitter tang to salads. Alternatively, allow the foliage to mature and eat lightly steamed.

Sow: late spring to early fall
Harvest: midsummer to late fall
◌ ☼ ☀

Chicory 'Sugar Loaf'
Treat in the same way as lettuce to produce tall, pale heads of crisp, bitter leaves or cut-and-come-again baby leaves. Chicory grows well in poorer soil, although watering may be required in dry spells.

Sow: mid-spring to late summer
Harvest: midsummer to mid-fall
◌ ☼ ☀

Swiss chard 'Bright Lights'
Multi-colored stems ranging from white and yellow to pink and purple make this a vibrant addition to the vegetable garden and flower border. Easy to grow, it reemerges in early spring if given winter protection.

Sow: mid-spring to midsummer
Harvest: early spring to mid-fall
◐ ◌ ☼

Swiss chard 'Charlotte'
One of the most attractive ruby chards, with bright red stems and contrasting green leaves veined a striking red. It looks fabulous in a pot or flower border, and the baby leaves liven up salads. A must for every garden.

Sow: mid-spring to midsummer
Harvest: at any time
◐ ◌ ☼

Swiss chard 'Lucullus'
Decorative and delicious, this chard rapidly produces generous crops of large green leaves on sturdy, pure white stems. Leaves and stems may be boiled, steamed, or stir-fried; their mild flavor is similar to beets.

Sow: mid-spring to midsummer
Harvest: early spring to mid-fall
◐ ◌ ☼

Cucurbits: zucchini, summer squash

Zucchini '*Zucchini*'
A reliable variety that forms a bushy plant, well suited to growing in a container. Zucchini with dark green skins and tasty pale flesh are produced in profusion from midsummer. Like all zucchini, they are best picked young.

Sow: mid-spring to early summer
Harvest: midsummer to early fall

Zucchini '*Defender*' F1
A phenomenally productive early variety. If harvested small, fruits will keep coming until mid-fall, and they are delicious. Plants are resistant to cucumber mosaic virus, which can cause other varieties to fail.

Sow: mid-spring to early summer
Harvest: midsummer to mid-fall

Zucchini '*Burpee's Golden*'
Another prolific zucchini variety that bears numerous decorative and delicious bright yellow fruits. The zucchini have a particularly fine flavor, especially when harvested small.

Sow: mid-spring to early summer
Harvest: midsummer to early fall

Zucchini '*Tromboncino*'
This vigorous Italian variety is best trained up a sunny wall to afford everyone a good view of its long, curved, bulbous-ended fruits. The pale green fruits can reach more than 12 in (30 cm) long.

Sow: mid-spring to early summer
Harvest: midsummer to early fall

Zucchini '*Venus*' F1
Unusually compact, these plants are great for containers or small gardens, and still produce ample crops of delicious, mid-green zucchini. In good conditions, fruits are ready to harvest 60 days after planting.

Sow: mid-spring to early summer
Harvest: early summer to mid-fall

Summer squash '*Long Green Bush*'
Despite its name, this variety forms quite a compact, bushy plant, making it suitable for the smaller garden. Long, deep green fruits, with pale green marrow stripes, swell rapidly, but can be picked as zucchini when small.

Sow: mid-spring to early summer
Harvest: midsummer to mid-fall

Cucurbits: squash, cucumbers

Squash *'Sunburst'* F1

A yellow "Patty Pan" variety, this squash has vibrant butter-colored fruits, shaped like flying saucers. Large crops of flavorsome fruits are produced by this easily grown variety if regular harvesting is carried out.

Sow: mid-spring to early summer
Harvest: midsummer to mid-fall
◊ ◗ ☼

Squash *'Uchiki Kuri'*

Also known as 'Red Kuri', this squash produces several medium-sized, bright orange fruits, with delicious, nutty, golden flesh. It performs particularly well in temperate climates. Fruits store well once cured.

Sow: mid- to late spring
Harvest: late summer to mid-fall
◊ ◗ ☼

Squash *'Pilgrim Butternut'* F1

A less vigorous and so more manageable butternut squash for the smaller garden. The semi-bush habit of the vine does not prevent a good crop of beige-skinned, orange-fleshed squashes, which store well.

Sow: mid- to late spring
Harvest: late summer to mid-fall
◊ ◗ ☼

Squash *'Crown Prince'* F1

This trailing squash is a favorite because of its exceptionally good nutty-flavored flesh. The steely gray skin of the fruits contrasts dramatically with the orange flesh and looks attractive on the vine.

Sow: mid-spring to late spring
Harvest: late summer to mid-fall
◊ ◗ ☼

Squash *'Turk's Turban'*

Not an exceptional culinary squash, with pale yellow flesh and a turnip-like flavor, but often grown for its ornamental qualities. The rich orange skin folds and forms a bulge splashed with green and cream.

Sow: mid- to late spring
Harvest: late summer to mid-fall
◊ ◗ ☼

Squash *'Festival'* F1

Ornamental and delicious, this trailing vine produces high yields of small, squat, orange and cream striped squashes, with sweet, nutty-tasting, cream flesh. The squashes are perfect for stuffing or baking, and store well.

Sow: mid- to late spring
Harvest: late summer to mid-fall
◊ ◗ ☼

Cucumber 'Bush Champion' F1
Grow this ridge cucumber outdoors—
its compact plants are ideal for small
gardens and pots, and have good
tolerance to cucumber mosaic virus.
The slightly knobby, dark green, sweet
fruits reach about 4 in (10 cm) long.

Sow: mid-spring to early summer
Harvest: late summer to mid-fall
○ ◑ ☀

Cucumber 'Marketmore'
An excellent, high-yielding cucumber,
producing sturdy, deep green fruit up
to 8 in (20 cm) long, with no bitterness.
This variety does well outdoors up a
wigwam or trellis. Resistance to
cucumber mosaic virus is a bonus.

Sow: mid-spring to early summer
Harvest: late summer to mid-fall
○ ◑ ☀

Cucumber 'Masterpiece'
Crisp, juicy, white flesh, under a deep
green, slightly spiny skin, makes this
ridge cucumber a good choice for
outdoor cultivation. This variety crops
reliably, but performs best when
allowed to climb.

Sow: mid-spring to early summer
Harvest: late summer to mid-fall
○ ◑ ☀

Cucumber 'Zeina' F1
An all-female variety that can be
grown in the greenhouse or outdoors.
Small, succulent, smooth-skinned
cucumbers can be harvested over a
long season and are a handy size to
eat at one meal.

Sow: early spring to early summer
Harvest: midsummer to mid-fall
○ ◑ ☀

Cucumber 'Petita' F1
For an abundance of juicy, miniature
cucumbers from the greenhouse, this
is the variety to choose. It is easy to
grow, even in difficult conditions, and
has all female flowers so bitter fruits
are not produced.

Sow: early spring to early summer
Harvest: midsummer to mid-fall
○ ◑ ☀

Cucumber 'Carmen' F1
Resistance to powdery mildew, scab,
and leaf spot makes this all-female
variety a good choice for greenhouse
cultivation. Impressive harvests of
straight, smooth, green fruits are
simple to produce.

Sow: early spring to early summer
Harvest: midsummer to mid-fall
○ ◑ ☀

Allium family: onions, shallots, green onions

Onion 'Ailsa Craig'

An old favorite, this reliable variety yields heavy crops of large, sweet onions, with smooth yellow-brown skin. Best sown as seed in spring to produce a good fall crop that stores well if allowed to dry.

Sow: late winter to early spring
Harvest: late summer to early fall
◊ ☼

Onion 'Sturon'

Traditionally grown from sets, this variety produces large, round, yellow-brown colored bulbs that have a strong skin, which makes them an excellent choice for winter storing. Seed is occasionally available.

Plant sets: late winter to early spring
Harvest: late summer to early fall
◊ ☼

Onion 'Red Baron'

Widely available as both seeds and sets, this variety has a rich red skin, with pronounced pink stripes between the bulb's layers. It will store for only a limited time.

Sow: late winter to mid-spring
Plant sets: early spring
Harvest: early to mid-fall
◊ ☼

Onion 'Senshyu'

Sets of this useful winter Japanese variety should be planted in fall and seeds sown a little before for an early summer harvest. The semi-flat, straw-colored bulbs grow to a good size and have a strong flavor.

Sow: late summer **Plant sets:** early to mid-fall.
Harvest: early to midsummer ◊ ☼

Onion 'Shakespeare'

For an early summer crop of globe-shaped onions with rich brown skins, try this British overwintering variety. The dense white flesh and sturdy skin mean that they store well, and they have an excellent flavor.

Sow: early to mid-fall
Harvest: early to midsummer
◊ ☼

Shallot 'Longor'

An attractive, elongated variety of shallot, with a pink flush to the skin and inner layers. The strongly flavored bulbs store well through fall and winter if carefully dried. Quicker to crop than traditional bulb onions.

Plant sets: late winter to mid-spring
Harvest: mid- to late summer
◊ ☼

Shallot 'Red Sun'

One of the most reliable red shallots, this variety has wonderful burgundy skin and white flesh with layers divided by pink rings. Appetizing chopped raw in salads, it is also well suited to cooking and pickling.

Plant sets: early to mid-spring
Harvest: mid- to late summer
◊ ☼

Shallot 'Golden Gourmet'

Large and yellow-skinned, this high-yielding variety produces bumper crops of good-quality bulbs from sets and is easy to store all through the winter. It is less prone to bolting in dry conditions than many shallots.

Plant sets: late winter to mid-spring
Harvest: mid- to late summer
◊ ☼

Green onion 'Paris Silverskin'

A dual-purpose small white onion that can be harvested young as a salad onion or left in the ground to bulb up for pickling. Easy to grow and compact, it makes an ideal crop for small gardens.

Sow: early to mid-spring
Harvest: mid- to late summer
◊ ☼

Green onion 'Guardsman'

This trusted, white-stemmed variety is extremely easy to grow. It is a good choice to sow successionally from spring to fall because it is hardy enough to overwinter and give an early spring crop. Resistant to white rot.

Sow: early spring to mid-fall
Harvest: late spring to mid-fall; late winter to early spring ◊ ☼

Green onion 'North Holland Blood Red'

An attractive variety with bold red bases and a mild flavor. Use thinnings from early sowings as green onions, leaving wider-spaced plants to develop into red-skinned maincrop onions.

Sow: early spring to early summer
Harvest: late spring to late summer
◊ ☼

Green onion 'White Lisbon'

A trusted old favorite, this variety produces white bulbs and bright green tops with a good, strong flavor. It is easy to grow but prone to downy mildew, so keep rows well spaced to avoid the spread of disease.

Sow: early spring to midsummer
Harvest: late spring to early fall
◊ ☼

Allium family: leeks, garlic

Leek 'Musselburgh'
An extremely hardy, sturdy leek, with a broad white stem topped by impressive green leaves, known as flags. This old variety can withstand the coldest winter, and can be harvested from late fall until late winter.

Sow: early to mid-spring
Harvest: late fall to late winter
◊ ☼

Leek 'Hannibal'
This handsome leek has deep green leaves and a long, white, straight stem. Suitable for fall and early winter cropping, it also produces impressive mini leeks when planted close together.

Sow: early to mid-spring
Harvest: early fall to early winter
◊ ☼

Leek 'Swiss Giant, Zermatt'
An elegant variety with a long, slender stem, which despite its name forms excellent mini leeks when planted at high densities. It is ready for harvest by late summer—an advantage for those with limited space in the garden.

Sow: early to mid-spring
Harvest: midsummer to late fall
◊ ☼

Garlic 'Solent Light'
One of the best garlics for cool climates, this is best planted in fall but also does well planted in spring. It matures in late summer and because it is a non-flowering, softneck type, stores extremely well.

Plant cloves: mid-fall to early spring
Harvest: midsummer to early fall ◊ ☼

Garlic 'Early Light'
This flowering, hardneck, purple-skinned variety is best used fresh but will store for about three months. The harvest will be eagerly anticipated, as this is one of the earliest varieties to crop in cool climates.

Plant cloves: mid-fall to midwinter
Harvest: late spring to early summer
◊ ☼

Garlic 'Elephant Garlic'
Closely related to the leek, this giant produces bulbs up to 4 in (10 cm) in diameter. Use the large, juicy cloves fresh from the soil to enjoy their mild, sweet flavor, which makes them particularly suitable for roasting.

Plant cloves: mid-fall to midwinter.
Harvest: midsummer to early fall
◊ ☼

Legumes: peas

Pea 'Feltham First'

Early and dwarf, this is a useful, high-yielding pea variety for small gardens. Better results are often achieved from fall sowings in containers, where plants are given some protection.

Sow: mid- to late fall; midwinter to early spring
Harvest: late spring to midsummer

Pea 'Twinkle'

An excellent early variety, the first sowings of which perform best if protected under cloches when young. Dwarf plants give good crops of full pods and have resistance to pea wilt and tolerance to downy mildew.

Sow: late winter to mid-spring
Harvest: late spring to midsummer

Pea 'Hurst Greenshaft'

Pairs of long pods develop high on these plants, making harvesting of this traditional variety's consistently large crops somewhat easier. The peas are large and sweet, and plants have good disease resistance.

Sow: early spring to early summer
Harvest: late spring to early fall

Pea 'Rondo'

One of the tastiest and heaviest cropping peas, this double-podded variety has dark green, straight pods up to 4 in (10 cm) long. Plants need supports, but the succulent peas should be ample reward.

Sow: early spring to early summer
Harvest: late spring to early fall

Pea 'Sugar Snap'

A versatile sugar snap variety that can be picked young and eaten whole, raw, or stir-fried, or harvested when mature and podded for fresh peas. Plants grow up to 6 ft (1.8 m) tall, so need support from trellis or canes.

Sow: early spring to early summer
Harvest: late spring to late summer

Pea 'Oregon Sugar Pod'

An excellent snow pea variety that produces wide, flat pods best eaten whole, either raw, steamed, or stir-fried. Expect large yields of these crisp, sweet pods from plants that grow to 36 in (90 cm).

Sow: early spring to early summer
Harvest: late spring to late summer

Legumes: beans

Runner bean *'Butler'*
This attractive, red-flowered runner bean grows vigorously and forms many long, stringless pods filled with pretty purple beans. They can be picked over a long season and, being stringless, are still palatable when a little larger.

Sow: mid-spring to early summer
Harvest: midsummer to mid-fall
🌢 🌢 ☼ ☼

Runner bean *'Liberty'*
A favorite with exhibitors, this runner bean has glorious scarlet flowers followed by extremely long (up to 18 in/45 cm) pods. The heavy crops of smooth-skinned pods are prized for their tasty, thick flesh.

Sow: mid-spring to early summer
Harvest: midsummer to mid-fall
🌢 🌢 ☼ ☼

Runner bean *'White Lady'*
The pure white flowers of this runner bean are thought to be less attractive to birds. Hot weather can prevent pods from setting on other varieties, but 'White Lady' still performs well, making it suitable for later sowings.

Sow: mid-spring to early summer
Harvest: midsummer to mid-fall
🌢 🌢 ☼ ☼

Runner bean *'Wisley Magic'*
A runner bean with bright red flowers that develop into slim pods up to 14 in (35 cm) long, with a delicious fresh flavor. The plants grow rapidly and produce good yields, but pods are not stringless so are best harvested young.

Sow: mid-spring to early summer
Harvest: midsummer to mid-fall
🌢 🌢 ☼ ☼

French bean *'Purple Queen'*
Perfect for a container or border, this compact dwarf French bean grows without supports and develops heavy crops of glossy, rich purple pods. The stringless pods have a fine flavor and turn green when cooked.

Sow: mid-spring to midsummer
Harvest: early summer to late fall
🌢 🌢 ☼ ☼

French bean *'Delinel'*
A dwarf bean for a bumper crop. In containers or beds, it produces large yields of rounded, long green beans with a firm texture and good flavor. Plants are resistant to common bean mosaic virus and anthracnose.

Sow: mid-spring to midsummer
Harvest: early summer to late fall
🌢 🌢 ☼ ☼

French bean 'The Prince'

This dwarf variety has long, flat, green pods, best harvested young when they are stringless. The flavor is excellent, and crops can be reliably harvested by early summer. They are also produced over a long period.

Sow: mid-spring to midsummer
Harvest: early summer to late fall
◐ ◊ ☼ ☀

French bean 'Ferrari'

A fine dwarf French bean—slim, succulent, bursting with flavor, and stringless. The plants do well sown in mid-spring if protected from frost and thrive in containers. The connoisseur's choice, as well as easy to grow.

Sow: mid-spring to midsummer
Harvest: early summer to late fall
◐ ◊ ☼ ☀

French bean 'Cobra'

Train up wigwams or trellis to achieve large crops of stringless, tender green beans, up to 8 in (20 cm) long. The flowers are an unusual shade of violet, which make the plants ornamental as well as productive.

Sow: mid-spring to midsummer
Harvest: early summer to late fall
◐ ◊ ☼ ☀

Borlotto 'Lingua di Fuoco'

Grown in the same way as a climbing French bean, this Italian borlotto bean has long, flattish, pale green pods marked with red. Eat whole when young or remove the purple-blotched seeds from mature pods and dry them.

Sow: mid-spring to midsummer
Harvest: early summer to late fall
◐ ◊ ☼

Broad bean 'Aquadulce Claudia'

An old favorite, this hardy broad bean can overwinter outdoors. Plants grow to 3 ft (90 cm) and yield a good crop of tender white beans in "cotton gauze" lined pods. Black bean aphid is often a pest on shoots.

Sow: mid- to late fall; mid- to late winter **Harvest:** late spring to early summer ◊ ☼

Broad bean 'The Sutton'

Compact and bushy, this broad bean reaches only 18 in (45 cm), so is ideal for small gardens and for sowing under cloches in late winter and on windy sites. It produces abundant small pods packed with juicy white beans.

Sow: midwinter to early spring
Harvest: early to late summer
◊ ☼

Fruiting vegetables: tomatoes

Tomato *'Totem'* F1
A dwarf upright bush variety that is the perfect size for patio containers and large window boxes. It crops well outdoors: by midsummer, its trusses are heavy with small, tasty red fruits.

Sow: (indoors) midwinter to mid-spring; (outdoors) early spring to mid-spring **Harvest:** midsummer to mid-fall ◊ ◑ ☼

Tomato *'Tumbler'* F1
Ideal outdoors in hanging baskets or large containers, this bush tomato has stems that trail attractively over the side of a pot. It provides a prolific crop of sweet, red cherry tomatoes.

Sow: (indoors) midwinter to mid-spring; (outdoors) early spring to mid-spring **Harvest:** midsummer to mid-fall ◊ ◑ ☼

Tomato *'Early Bush Cherry'*
Easy to grow and quick to ripen, this bush variety does well outdoors in containers, or in a greenhouse. Its huge numbers of small, round, cherrylike fruits have a sweet flavor.

Sow: (indoors) midwinter to mid-spring; (outdoors) early spring to mid-spring **Harvest:** midsummer to mid-fall ◊ ◑ ☼

Tomato *'Sungold'* F1
Masses of incredibly sweet, orange cherry tomatoes make this a popular variety. It is a cordon tomato, so needs staking and side-shooting. It grows well under glass or outdoors.

Sow: (indoors) midwinter to mid-spring; (outdoors) early spring to mid-spring **Harvest:** midsummer to mid-fall ◊ ◑ ☼

Tomato *'Sweet Olive'* F1
For baby plum tomatoes that grow outdoors, try this reliable cordon variety. The clusters of scarlet fruits have an excellent, intense flavor, and the skins do not split readily. Plants may require some staking.

Sow: early to mid-spring **Harvest:** midsummer to mid-fall ◊ ◑ ☼

Tomato *'Shirley'* F1
This dependable greenhouse variety yields heavy crops of large, rounded, scarlet fruits, even in poor weather conditions. A cordon variety, it requires staking and side-shooting, but has some disease resistance.

Sow: midwinter to early spring **Harvest:** early summer to early fall ◊ ◑ ☼

Tomato *'Tigerella'* **F1**
Unusual red fruits striped with yellow make this variety stand out, but they also taste delicious and mature early. A cordon tomato that crops well indoors and outside.

Sow: (indoors) midwinter to mid-spring; (outdoors) early spring to mid-spring **Harvest:** midsummer to mid-fall ◊ ◓ ☼

Tomato *'Gardener's Delight'*
Perfect for a sheltered spot outside or a greenhouse, this is an extremely popular cordon tomato variety because of its bumper crops of fine-flavored, large cherry tomatoes.

Sow: (indoors) midwinter to mid-spring; (outdoors) early to mid-spring **Harvest:** midsummer to mid-fall ◊ ◓ ☼

Tomato *'Ferline'* **F1**
An excellent cordon tomato producing large, rounded, red fruits, with increased blight tolerance. Plants grow well inside or out, and the fruits have a rich flavor.

Sow: (indoors) midwinter to mid-spring; (outdoors) early to mid-spring **Harvest:** midsummer to mid-fall ◊ ◓ ☼

Tomato *'Supersweet 100'* **F1**
For long trusses of juicy, sugary, scarlet fruits, this is a great variety to try under glass. With good resistance to verticillium wilt, these vigorous cordon plants are easy to grow and yield reliably generous crops.

Sow: midwinter to mid-spring **Harvest:** midsummer to mid-fall ◊ ◓ ☼

Tomato *'Super Marmande'*
This variety has a bushy habit, but benefits from some support. The large fleshy, puckered fruits are bursting with flavor and are a favorite in France. Plants thrive outdoors in warm areas.

Sow: midwinter to mid-spring **Harvest:** midsummer to mid-fall ◊ ◓ ☼

Tomato *'Summer Sweet'* **F1**
An early plum tomato for a sunny spot outdoors or in a greenhouse, this cordon variety yields plenty of small, tasty, red fruits over a long season. Plants have resistance to fusarium to help ensure a good crop.

Sow: midwinter to mid-spring **Harvest:** midsummer to mid-fall ◊ ◓ ☼

Fruiting vegetables: eggplant, peppers, sweet corn

Eggplant 'Moneymaker' F1

This is one of the most dependable eggplants in cool climates. The upright plants look good in containers, and while the best long, dark purple fruits are achieved under glass, plants also do well in a sunny outdoor spot.

Sow: early to mid-spring
Harvest: midsummer to early fall
○ ◗ ☼

Eggplant 'Black Beauty'

A prolific variety, producing many glossy, deep purple, oval-shaped fruits. The highest yields are achieved with the protection of a greenhouse. Plants are best tied to supports to help bear the weight of the fruits.

Sow: early to mid-spring
Harvest: midsummer to early fall
○ ◗ ☼

Eggplant 'Mohican'

With its compact bushy habit and immaculate white fruits, this eggplant makes a striking container plant for a sunny patio or greenhouse. Plants reach only 24 in (60 cm). Pick the fruits small to increase the yield.

Sow: early to mid-spring
Harvest: midsummer to early fall
◗ ○ ☼

Pepper 'Gypsy' F1

Good, early crops are reliably produced by this sweet pepper, which performs well under glass. Tapering fruits ripen to bright red from yellow-green and have thick, succulent flesh. Plants are resistant to tobacco mosaic virus.

Sow: early to mid-spring
Harvest: midsummer to mid-fall
○ ☼

Pepper 'Marconi Rosso'

The elongated fruits of this pepper are best eaten when red, because at this stage they are extremely sweet and ideal for roasting. Plants are high-yielding indoors or in a warm, sunny spot outside.

Sow: early to mid-spring
Harvest: midsummer to mid-fall
○ ☼

Pepper 'Corno di Torro Rosso'

Delicious, long, thin-walled peppers are sweet once they have turned to purple and red. This early variety appreciates the extra heat in a greenhouse, but crops outdoors in warm areas.

Sow: early to mid-spring
Harvest: midsummer to mid-fall
○ ☼

Pepper 'Hungarian Hot Wax'

An attractive, compact chili pepper bearing tapering fruits that are sweet and yellow when young, but hot and bright red when mature. The best crops are achieved with the protection of a greenhouse or large cloches.

Sow: early to mid-spring
Harvest: midsummer to mid-fall
◊ ☼

Pepper 'Prairie Fire'

These tiny, bullet-shaped chilies are extremely fiery and look decorative pointing up from the bushy plants, which reach no more than 8 in (20 cm) tall. Ideal for windowsills or against a sunny wall. Plants crop heavily.

Sow: early to mid-spring
Harvest: midsummer to mid-fall
◊ ☼

Pepper 'Friar's Hat'

Best grown in a greenhouse, these tall plants produce heavy yields of bizarre chilies shaped like floppy sun hats. Plants need staking, while fruits need a long, hot growing season to ripen and build up a hot chili flavor.

Sow: early to mid-spring
Harvest: midsummer to mid-fall
◊ ☼

Sweet corn 'Butterscotch' F1

A super-sweet mid-season variety, forming large cobs up to 8 in (20 cm) long that are filled with tender, sugary, butter yellow kernels. Grows vigorously and crops well even in cool weather conditions.

Sow: mid- to late spring
Harvest: late summer to early fall
◊ ☼

Sweet corn 'Indian Summer'

These spectacular multicolored cobs have sweet-tasting kernels in shades of yellow, cream, red, and purple. Keep the plants separate from other sweet corn varieties to prevent cross-pollination and maintain the colors.

Sow: mid- to late spring
Harvest: late summer to mid-fall
◊ ☼

Sweet corn 'Lark' F1

This variety consistently produces a high proportion of healthy seedlings from each sowing, and is ideal for beginners. The sweet, tender cobs are delicious when boiled briefly and topped with melted butter.

Sow: mid- to late spring
Harvest: late summer to mid-fall
◊ ☼

Asparagus *'Connover's Colossal'*
A traditional variety that yields a heavy crop of thick green spears early in the season. Buy young crowns and try not to harvest in their first year—just cut a few spears in the second and reap the reward in the third.

Plant: late winter to early spring
Harvest: late spring
◊ ☼

Jerusalem artichoke *'Fuseau'*
This relative of the sunflower produces long, smooth tubers, with a flavor similar to globe artichokes, which are usually eaten cooked. Plants may reach 10 ft (3 m) in height, each yielding about 10 tubers.

Plant: late winter to late spring
Harvest: early to late winter
◊ ◐ ☼ ☀

Globe artichoke *'Green Globe'*
Often difficult to find in stores, but easy to grow, this reliable globe variety has large flowerheads with delicious, tender hearts. Grow from offsets where available.

Sow: late winter to early spring
Plant offsets: late spring to early summer **Harvest:** late spring to early summer ◊ ◐ ☼ ☀

Celeriac *'Monarch'*
Easier to grow than celery, with a milder flavor, celeriac is delicious raw, steamed, or roasted. This cultivar has unusually smooth skin, making it easier to clean than most, and has fine-textured, creamy flesh.

Sow: early to mid-spring
Harvest: mid- to late fall
◊ ◐ ☼ ☀

Celery *'Victoria'* **F1**
The attractive pale green stems of this variety have a particularly good flavor and crispness. There is no need to earth up the stalks to blanch them, and the plants are slow to bolt.

Sow: late winter to mid-spring
Harvest: late summer to mid-fall
◊ ◐ ☼

Celery *'Celebrity'* **F1**
An excellent self-blanching variety that grows equally well outdoors or in a greenhouse. The light green stems have a delicious, strong flavor, and plants resist bolting well.

Sow: late winter to mid-spring.
Harvest: late summer to mid-fall
◊ ◐ ☼

Herbs

Parsley 'Plain Leaved 2'

A fine French parsley, with soft, flat, rich green leaves that have a good, strong flavor. Easily grown as an annual indoors or outside, although parsley is biennial and hardy enough to persist in most gardens.

Sow: early spring to late summer
Harvest: year round

Parsley 'Envy'

Handsome and vigorous, this variety produces a mass of tightly curled, bright green, full-flavored leaves. Parsley seeds may be slow to germinate, but be sure that the soil is soaked after sowing.

Sow: early spring to late summer
Harvest: year round

Basil 'Sweet Genovese'

Large-leaved and intensely aromatic, this is the basil to use in Italian dishes. The tender plants will grow in a sunny spot outdoors, but often do best on a bright windowsill or in a greenhouse. Pinch out young leaves regularly.

Sow: early spring to midsummer
Harvest: year round

Basil 'Magic Mountain'

With its glossy, purple-tinted foliage and tall spikes of lilac flowers, this tender herb makes a pretty garden plant in its own right. The leaves have a delicate aniseed scent, which makes them suitable for Thai cooking.

Sow: early spring to midsummer
Harvest: year round

Thyme 'Silver Posie'

The tiny gray and cream leaves of this compact and low-growing thyme are intensely fragrant, complementing the flavors of chicken and fish. An evergreen hardy perennial, it has clusters of pink flowers in summer.

Sow: early to late spring
Harvest: year round

Thyme 'Doone Valley'

The vibrant yellow variegation of this thyme's evergreen foliage, combined with a flush of purple summer flowers, makes it a beautiful plant for a pot or herb garden. The lemon-scented leaves taste good with fish or in stews.

Sow: early to late spring
Harvest: year round

Herbs and sprouting seeds

Oregano (*Origanum vulgare*)
A pungent Mediterranean herb often used in Italian cuisine and reliably perennial in freely draining soil. Its rounded, yellow-green leaves and low-growing habit make it an attractive garden plant, useful for edging paths.

Sow: early to late spring
Harvest: year round
◊ ☼

Rosemary (*Rosmarinus officinalis*)
This shrub bears the tough, narrow, strongly scented leaves that combine so well with lamb. As an evergreen, rosemary provides useful structure in the herb or vegetable garden, and can be pruned to maintain its shape.

Sow: early to late spring
Harvest: year round
◊ ☼

Fennel (*Foeniculum vulgare*)
Elegant and airy, fennel comes in green and bronze forms and may reach 6 ft (1.8 m) tall. It is a good-looking perennial in ornamental borders, where its aniseed-flavored leaves, and later its seeds, can be harvested as required.

Sow: early to late spring
Harvest: late spring to early fall
◊ ☼

Apple mint (*Mentha suaveolens*)
Delicious, but invasive, this mint is best confined to a pot in small gardens. It is perennial and each spring sends up new shoots clothed with soft, furry, sweetly minty leaves, perfect for cooking with new potatoes.

Sow: early to late spring
Harvest: late spring to late summer
◊ ◖ ☼

Spearmint (*Mentha spicata*)
Spearmint's clean, crisp flavor is ideal for adding to salads, desserts, and drinks. The pointed, deep green leaves are glossy and appealing, but this is also an invasive perennial, so keep its spreading shoots in check.

Sow: early to late spring
Harvest: late spring to early fall
◊ ◖ ☼

Chives (*Allium schoenoprasum*)
The clumps of these easy-to-grow perennials have spiky leaves topped with purple pompon flowers, making them an excellent path edging. The delicate onion flavor of chives suits soups, salads, and quiches.

Sow: early to late spring
Harvest: at any time
◊ ☼ ☼

Cilantro 'Cilantro for Leaf'

A lush, leafy annual, bred to yield several cuts of spicy leaves, rather than seeds. Sow successively every six weeks to ensure a constant supply and keep plants well watered to stop them from rapidly running to seed.

Sow: mid-spring to early fall
Harvest: early spring to early fall
◊ ☼

Common sage (*Salvia officinalis*)

Ornamental, with many culinary uses, this aromatic shrub has pale green leaves covered in an attractive gray down. Encourage bushy growth by pinching out growing tips, but replace old plants every five years.

Sow: mid- to late spring
Harvest: at any time
◊ ☼

Lemon grass (*Cymbopogon citratus*)

Tropical and tender, this grass needs to be kept above 45°F (7°C) in winter. The stout, citrus-scented stems can be slow to bulk up in cool climates, but form clumps from which stems can be separated and used in Thai dishes.

Sow: mid- to late spring
Harvest: late spring to early fall
◊ ☼

Alfalfa

A nutritious, crisp sprout, with a slightly nutty flavor, alfalfa is delicious in salads and sandwiches. Soaking the seeds for eight hours before sprouting helps speed up the process. Sprouts should be ready from trays or jars in 4–5 days.

Sow: at any time
Harvest: at any time

Mung beans

These tiny green beans burst rapidly into life to become the well-known white Chinese bean sprouts, so often included in stir-fries. Soak the beans for 8–12 hours, before sprouting in a jar, tray, or sprouting bag for 2–5 days.

Sow: at any time
Harvest: at any time

Garbanzos

Sprouted garbanzos (chickpeas) are a tasty snack or addition to a salad and require only 2–3 days in a jar, tray, or sprouting bag before they are ready to eat. Soak them in water for 8–12 hours before sprouting, to ensure that the seed coat is softened.

Sow: at any time
Harvest: at any time

Suppliers

Vegetable seeds & plants

Baker Creek Heirloom Seed Co.
2278 Baker Creek Road
Mansfield, MO 65704
www.rareseeds.com

Cross Country Nurseries
PO Box 170
Rosemont, NJ 08556
www.chileplants.com

J.L. Hudson, Seedsman
Star Route 2, Box 337
La Honda, CA 94020
www.jlhudsonseeds.net

Johnny's Selected Seeds
955 Benton Avenue
Winslow, ME 04901
www.johnnyseeds.com

Nourse Farms
41 River Road
South Deerfield, MA 01373
www.noursefarms.com

Renee's Garden Seeds
7389 West Zayante Road
Felton, CA 95018
www.reneesgarden.com

Sand Hill Preservation Center
1878 230th St
Calamus, IA 52729
www.sandhillpreservation.com

Stokes Seeds
PO Box 548
Buffalo, NY 14240
www.stokeseeds.com

Swallowtail Garden Seeds
122 Calistoga Road #178
Santa Rosa, CA 95409
www.swallowtailgardenseeds.com

The Tasteful Garden
973 County Road 8
Heflin, AL 36264
www.tastefulgarden.com

Territorial Seed Company
PO Box 158
Cottage Grove, OR 97424
www.territorial-seed.com

Thompson & Morgan
220 Faraday Ave
Jackson, NJ 08527
www.thompson-morgan.com

Underwood Gardens (Grandma's Garden Catalog)
1414 Zimmerman Rd
Woodstock, IL 60098
www.underwoodgardens.com

ValueSeeds.com
PO Box 580
Jackson, NJ 08527
www.valueseeds.com

Victory Seed Company
PO Box 192
Molalla, OR 97038
www.victoryseeds.com

Greenhouses & supplies

ACF Greenhouses
380 Greenhouse Drive
Buffalo Junction, VA 24529
www.littlegreenhouse.com

Charley's Greenhouse and Garden Supply
79 State Route 536
Mt. Vernon, WA 98273
www.charleysgreenhouse.com

FarmTek Growers Supply
1440 Field of Dreams Way
Dyersville, IA 52040
www.farmtek.com

Pest control

Extremely Green Gardening Company
953 Islington Street
Portsmouth, NH 03801
www.extremelygreen.com

Harmony Farm Supply & Nursery
3244 Hwy. 116 North
Sebastopol, CA 95472
www.harmonyfarm.com

The Natural Gardening Company
PO Box 750776
Petaluma, CA 94975
www.naturalgardening.com

Peaceful Valley Farm Supply
PO Box 2209
Grass Valley, CA 95945
www.groworganic.com

Rohde's Nursery & Nature Store
1651 Wall St.
Garland, TX 75041
www.beorganic.com

Irrigation systems

Arid Solutions, Inc.
34 Paseo de Paz
Tijeras, NM 87059
www.aridsolutionsinc.com

The Drip Store
1145 Linda Vista Drive, Ste. 108
San Marcos, CA 92078
www.dripirrigation.com

DripWorks
190 Sanhedrin Circle
Willits, CA 95490
www.dripworksusa.com

Mr. Drip
PO Box 609
Concho, AZ 85924
www.mrdrip.com

Composting

Composters.com
32 Rancho Circle
Lake Forest, CA 92630
www.composters.com

Wormman's Worm Farm
PO Box 6947
Monroe Township, NJ 08831
www.wormman.com

Index

Index

Acknowledgments

The publisher would like to thank the following for their kind permission to reproduce their photographs:

(Key: a-above; b-below/bottom; c-center; f-far; l-left; r-right; t-top)

1–2 Airedale: Sarah Cuttle. **4** Mike Newton (c). **5** Airedale: Sarah Cuttle (t). **6–7** Airedale: Sarah Cuttle. **8** Airedale: Sarah Cuttle (tr); Amanda Jensen: Designer: Alan Capper with Kent Allan, Kent Design and Ross Allan Designs for Garden Africa, Chelsea Flower Show 2006 (tl); Amanda Jensen, Chelsea Flower Show 2006 (b). **9** Mark Bolton: Designer: Kate Frey, Fetzer Vineyards/Chelsea Flower Show 2005. **10–11** Mike Newton (t). Airedale: Sarah Cuttle (b). **11** Airedale: David Murphy (t); Amanda Jensen: Designer: Paul Stone, Mayor of London's Office, The Sunshine Garden, Hampton Court 2006 (b). **12–13** Garden World Images: Matt Keal/Eden Project. **13** Mark Bolton: Nicky Daw, Lower House, Powys (t). Airedale: Amanda Jensen (b). **14** Airedale: Sarah Cuttle (t). Mark Bolton: Goram, Teasdale, Thornbury, Glos. (r). **15** Airedale: Sarah Cuttle: Designers: Darren Rudge & H Wood, City of Wolverhampton College/Gardeners' World Live 2006. **16** Airedale: Sarah Cuttle (t). **16–17** Mark Bolton: Andy Luft, Nailsea, Somerset. **17** Airedale: Sarah Cuttle: Nottingham Trent University/Gardeners' World Live 2006 (tl); Designers: Darren Rudge & H Wood, City of Wolverhampton College/Gardeners' World Live 2006 (r). **18** Mark Bolton. **19** RHS *The Garden*: Tim Sandall (t). Airedale: Sarah Cuttle (bl); Amanda Jensen (br). **22** Airedale: Sarah Cuttle (l). DK Images: Peter Anderson (r). **23** Airedale: David Murphy (l); Amanda Jensen: Designer: Paul Stone, Mayor of London's Office, The Sunshine Garden, Hampton Court 2006 (r). **28** DK Images: Peter Anderson. **29** Airedale: Sarah Cuttle (tl) (bl) (br). DK Images: Peter Anderson (tr). **30** Airedale: David Murphy. **31** Airedale: Amanda Jensen (t). **32** Airedale: Sarah Cuttle (br). DK Images: Peter Anderson (t) (bl). **33** DK Images: Peter Anderson (tl) (cl) (cr) (bl) (br). **34** DK Images: Peter Anderson. **35** DK Images: Peter Anderson (tl) (b). **36** Airedale: David Murphy. **37** Airedale: Sarah Cuttle (bl). **38** Airedale: Sarah Cuttle. **39** DK Images: Peter Anderson (t) (bl). Airedale: Sarah Cuttle (br). **42** Airedale: Sarah Cuttle. **43** Airedale: Sarah Cuttle (tl). Thompson & Morgan (fbr). **44** Airedale: Suttons Seeds (fbr). Thompson & Morgan (bl). **46** Airedale: Sarah Cuttle. **47** Airedale: Sarah Cuttle (tr) (fbr). Chase Organics Ltd (fbl). **49** Airedale: David Murphy (tl); Sarah Cuttle (br) (fbr). DK Images: Peter

Anderson (tr). **50** Airedale: Sarah Cuttle. **51** Airedale: Sarah Cuttle (tl) (br). **52** Airedale: Sarah Cuttle. **53** Airedale: Sarah Cuttle (br). Chase Organics Ltd (fbr). **54** Airedale: Sarah Cuttle. **55** Airedale: Sarah Cuttle (fbl) (bl). **58** Airedale: Sarah Cuttle. **60** Airedale: Sarah Cuttle. **64** Airedale: Sarah Cuttle. **66** Airedale: David Murphy. **68** Airedale: Sarah Cuttle. **82** Airedale: Sarah Cuttle. **84** Airedale: David Murphy. **85** Airedale: Sarah Cuttle (tl) (tr) (bl). **86** Airedale: Sarah Cuttle (t) (br). DK Images: Peter Anderson (bl). **87** DK Images: Peter Anderson (t). **88–89** Airedale: David Murphy. **90** Airedale: Sarah Cuttle (cr). DK Images: Peter Anderson (tr). Thompson & Morgan (tl). **91** RHS *The Garden*: Tim Sandall. **92** Airedale: Sarah Cuttle (tl). Suttons Seeds (cr). DT Brown (bl). **93** Airedale: David Murphy. **94** Malcolm Dodds (tl). **96** Airedale: Sarah Cuttle (br). DK Images: Peter Anderson (bl). Derek St Romaine (tl). **97** Derek St Romaine: RHS Garden Rosemoor. **98–99** Airedale: Sarah Cuttle. **100** Airedale: Sarah Cuttle (tl) (br). **101** Airedale: Sarah Cuttle. **102** Airedale: Sarah Cuttle (br). Thompson & Morgan (cl). **103** DK Images: Steve Wooster. **106** Airedale: Sarah Cuttle. **107** Airedale: David Murphy (tl); Sarah Cuttle (ca). DK Images: Peter Anderson (cb). **108** Airedale: Sarah Cuttle (bl) (br). **109** DK Images: Mark Winwood (tl); Peter Anderson (bl). **110** DK Images: Deni Bown (c); Peter Anderson (ca) (tr) (cr) (bc). Airedale: David Murphy (cl). **111** Airedale: Sarah Cuttle (bc) (br). DK Images: Deni Bown (tr) (c) (bl). Malcolm Dodds (tl). **112** Airedale: Sarah Cuttle (bl) (bc). DK Images: Peter Anderson (br). **113** DK Images: Peter Anderson (c) (cr) (bc). Photoshot/NHPA: N A Callow (bl). **114** DK Images: Peter Anderson (tr) (br). Airedale: David Murphy (bl). **115** Airedale: David Murphy (tl). DK Images: Peter Anderson (cl) (bl). **116** Airedale: Sarah Cuttle. **117** Airedale: David Murphy (tl) (br); Sarah Cuttle (tr). DK Images: Peter Anderson (bl). **118** Airedale: Sarah Cuttle. **119** Airedale: Sarah Cuttle (br). **121** DK Images: Peter Anderson (r). **122–123** Airedale: David Murphy. **124** Thompson & Morgan (bl). **125** Airedale: Sarah Cuttle (tc) (br). Thompson & Morgan (tl). DT Brown (tr). **126** Thompson & Morgan (tr). Fothergills (tl) (bl). **127** Airedale: Sarah Cuttle (tr). Suttons Seeds (br). Thompson & Morgan (bc). Fothergills (bl). **128** Airedale: Sarah Cuttle (bc). Suttons Seeds (tl) (tr). Fothergills (tc). **129** Airedale: Sarah Cuttle (bl). Chase Organics Ltd (tl) (tc). Thompson & Morgan (bc) (br). Fothergills (tr). **130** Airedale: Sarah Cuttle (tr). Thompson & Morgan (tl) (bl). DT Brown (tc) (br). Fothergills (bc). **131** Airedale: Sarah Cuttle (tc). Suttons Seeds (tl). Thompson & Morgan (tr)

(br). Fothergills (bl). **132** Suttons Seeds (br). DT Brown (bc). **133** Chase Organics Ltd (tl). Thompson & Morgan (tc). DT Brown (tr). **134** Airedale: Sarah Cuttle (tl); David Murphy (bl); Mike Newton (tr). Fothergills (tc) (bc) (br). **135** Airedale: Sarah Cuttle (tl) (tr) (bl). Thompson & Morgan (bc). DT Brown (br). Fothergills (tc). **136** (bl). DT Brown (tr) (bc). **137** Airedale: Sarah Cuttle (tr) (bc). Marshalls Seeds (tl). Thompson & Morgan (tc). **138** Marshalls Seeds (bl) (br). Joy Michaud/Sea Spring Photos (tc). W. Robinson & Son Ltd. (bc). DT Brown (tl). Fothergills (tr). **139** Airedale: Sarah Cuttle (tr) (br). Joy Michaud/Sea Spring Photos (tc). DT Brown (tl) (bc). **140** Airedale: Sarah Cuttle (tc). Thompson & Morgan (bl) (bc) (br). Fothergills (tl). **141** Airedale: Sarah Cuttle (tc). Chase Organics (tl). Thompson & Morgan (br). DT Brown (tr) (bl) (bc). **142** Airedale: Sarah Cuttle (tc) (tr) (bl). Joy Michaud/Sea Spring Photos (tl). **143** Airedale: Sarah Cuttle (tc). Marshalls Seeds (tr). DT Brown (bc). Fothergills (tl) (bl) (br). **144** Suttons Seeds (bc). Thompson & Morgan (tr). Fothergills (tl). **145** Marshalls Seeds (bc) (br). Thompson & Morgan (tl) (tr). **146** DT Brown (br). **147** Airedale: Sarah Cuttle (tr) (bc). Chase Organics (bl). DT Brown (tl) (tc). **148** Airedale: Sarah Cuttle (tl) (bl). Thompson & Morgan (tr). DT Brown (tc). Fothergills (bc). **149** Airedale: Sarah Cuttle (br). Thompson & Morgan (bl). Fothergills (tl) (tc) (bc). **150** Airedale: Sarah Cuttle (tl) (tr). DT Brown (tc). **151** DT Brown (tl). **152** Airedale: Sarah Cuttle (tl) (bl) (bc). DT Brown (br). **153** Airedale: Sarah Cuttle (tc).

All other images © Dorling Kindersley. For further information, see www.dkimages.com

Every effort has been made to trace the copyright holders. We apologize in advance for any unintentional omission and would be pleased to insert the appropriate acknowledgments in any subsequent edition.

Dorling Kindersley would also like to thank the following: *Editors for Airedale Publishing:* Helen Ridge, Fiona Wild, Mandy Lebentz *Designer for Airedale Publishing:* Murdo Culver. *Index:* Michèle Clarke

Airedale Publishing would like to thank the following: DT Brown; Bryants Nurseries; Chase Organics; Mr Fothergill's; Marshalls/Unwins; Northern Polytunnels; Strulch; Suttons Seeds; Thompson & Morgan.